The Anxiety First Aid Kit

Quick Tools For Extreme, Uncertain Times

Various Authors

16pt

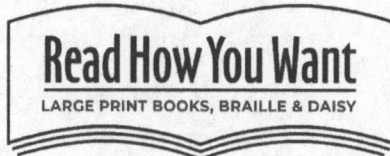

Read How You Want
LARGE PRINT BOOKS, BRAILLE & DAISY

Copyright Page from the Original Book

Library of Congress Cataloging-in-Publication Data on file

TABLE OF CONTENTS

INTRODUCTION i
PART I: FINDING CALM RIGHT AWAY 1
   1: DON'T BE ALARMED 1
   2: NOTICE YOU'RE ALL RIGHT, RIGHT NOW 7
   3: DIAPHRAGMATIC BREATHING 12
   4: CREATE YOUR SPECIAL PLACE 17
   5: TAKE REFUGE 21
   6: PROGRESSIVE RELAXATION 25
   7: SITTING MEDITATION 28
   8: RAPID RELAXATION 31
   9: RELAXING VISUALIZATION 34
   10: FEEL SAFER 40
PART II: FACING WORRY AND ANXIETY 45
   11: CHANGE YOUR INTERPRETATIONS 45
   12: TAKE YOUR WORRIES FOR A WALK 48
   13: REPLACE THOUGHTS 52
   14: MAKE A WORRY APPOINTMENT 55
   15: CHANGE THE ANXIETY CHANNEL 60
   16: PUT YOUR WORRIES IN A LINEUP 64
   17: DO THE OPPOSITE 67
   18: COUNT YOUR WORRIES 70
   19: HUMOR YOUR WORRY 74
   20: THE WORRY EXPERIMENT 78
   21: REPLACE WORRY WITH PLANNING 82
PART III: ADVANCED RELAXATION SKILLS 85
   22: THE MINDFULNESS POWER UP 85
   23: THE PENDULUM DROP 89
   24: FIVE-FINGER EXERCISE 93
   25: AUTOGENICS 97
   26: ANTI-STRESS COMBOS 103
   27: TAKE IN THE GOOD 107

PART IV: SUPER EFFECTIVE STRATEGIES THAT TAKE
A LITTLE MORE TIME   113
   28: SEE THE GOOD IN YOURSELF   113
   29: THINK THE THOUGHT—WITH A TWIST   118
   30: GET EXCITED   121
   31: COGNITIVE DEFUSION   126
   32: BEAT EXHAUSTION AND FIND STRENGTH   131
   33: USE EXERCISE TO COPE WITH ANXIETY   135
   34: GET SOME SLEEP   139
   35: SEND ANXIETY TO THE SPAM FOLDER   145
   36: COPING THOUGHTS   149
   37: BE GENEROUS   153
   38: LOVE   159
   39: ACKNOWLEDGE AND ACCEPT   163
   40: HAVE FAITH   168
SUGGESTED READING   173
BACK COVER MATERIAL   182

INTRODUCTION

These are extreme and uncertain times. From natural disasters to downsizing and automation to global pandemics that previously seemed unimaginable—not to mention political division about all of the above—we have more than enough to worry about.

When picking up this book, you likely sought relief from the burden of racing thoughts, obsessive thinking about worst case scenarios, or the nervous "always-on" feeling that anxiety leaves in your body. This book will help you feel better, but it is important to know that your feelings are valid. Even on good days, it can be hard *not* to feel like disaster is right around the corner and that we need to do everything we can to be ready for it.

As for bad days ... we believe that this book can help. Just like the first aid kit stashed under the bathroom sink, this mental health toolkit can give you a welcome respite from panic and worry about the future so that you can focus on what you can do in the here and now.

In this short book, we have compiled forty of the easiest and most effective anxiety-reducing exercises, techniques, and practices from top mental health experts, all of whom have put these skills into practice with clients. In addition, all of these techniques come from evidence-based treatments. By "evidence-based," we don't just mean that the tools in this book have worked for decades with hundreds of clients—they have—but also that they have been tested and approved in research labs all over the world.

Perhaps you have heard about cognitive behavioral therapy, mindfulness-based stress reduction, or neuroscience. If you have, then you might have a sense of how this book will help you. If you haven't, don't worry. Knowing these therapies is not important when it comes getting the most out of this book. In these pages, we want you to focus on improving your mood, getting a better understanding of your thoughts, and making sure you are living in accordance with what really matters to you. But we've also included a short suggested reading list at the end of this book for those interested in learning more about any of these therapies.

This book starts by teaching you techniques to calm down before you start working on the more difficult work of managing anxious thoughts and feelings. If you're able, we recommend working through it from beginning to end, because it's easier to work on your anxiety once you've established a baseline of calm, or non-reactivity.

This book is also designed to get you what you need when you need it, so there's no need to try all of the relaxation techniques if you already know what works for you. Similarly, if as you practice you find that exercise 9, "Relaxing Visualization," for example, works well for you, simply make it a habit and move on to the next part. All of the techniques in this book can be used in a moment's notice—as needed and on demand. They are flexible enough to work with any kind of anxious thought or worry, so feel free to jump in and out. Perhaps leaving the book on the coffee table—or somewhere else where it is readily available—can help you find relief when you need it.

As you move through the book, try to bring whatever amount of playfulness you can to these exercises and techniques. It is important to keep an open mind. That said, if something doesn't feel like it is working for you, drop it and move on to something else. In this book, you are the priority.

These times truly are distressing, but finding a moment to take care of your mental health doesn't have to be. With that, let's take a deep breath and get started.

PART I

FINDING CALM RIGHT AWAY

1

DON'T BE ALARMED

What to Know

The nervous system has been evolving for about 600 million years. During all this time, creatures—worms, crabs, lizards, rats, monkeys, hominids, humans—that were real mellow, watching the sunlight on the leaves, getting all Zen, absorbed in inner peace ... *CHOMP* got eaten because they didn't notice the shadow overhead or crackle of twigs nearby.

The ones that survived to pass on their genes were fearful and vigilant—and we are their great-great-grand-children, bred to be afraid. Even though we've come a long way from the Serengeti, we're still quick to feel unsettled in any situation that seems the least bit threatening. Even if the situations you're in are reasonably good, there are other, innate sources of alarm rooted in our biology. Basically, to survive, animals—including us—must continually try to:

- Separate themselves from the world.
- Stabilize many dynamic systems in the body, mind, relationships, and environment.
- Get rewards and avoid harms.

But here's the problem. Each of these strategies flies in the face of some basic facts about existence:

- Everything is connected to everything else, so it's impossible to fundamentally separate self and world.
- As you've likely noticed: everything changes, so it's impossible to keep things stable in the body, mind, relationships, or environment.
- Rewards are fleeting, costly, or unobtainable, and some harms are inevitable. So it's impossible to hold

onto pleasure forever and totally escape pain.

Alarms sound whenever we run into trouble practicing one of these strategies, which is many times a day (especially in times of chaos in the world), because of the contradictions between the nature of existence and what we must do to survive. These alarms create a background of unease, irritability, caution, and pessimism; the ones you're consciously aware of are emotionally and often physically uncomfortable—such as anxiety, anger, or pain.

Don't underestimate the amount of background alarm in your body and mind right now. It's hardwired and relentless, inherent in the collision between the needs of life and the realities of existence. While this alarmism has been a great strategy for keeping creatures alive to pass on their genes, it's not good for your health, well-being, relationships, or ambitions. Threat signals are usually way out of proportion to what is actually happening. They make you pull in your wings and play safe and small, and cling tighter to "us" and fear "them." At the level of groups and nations, our vulnerability to alarm makes us easy to manipulate with fear.

What to Do

1. Take a stand for yourself. You might even say, "I'm tired of being needlessly afraid." Consider the price you've paid over the past few months: the running for cover, the muzzling of self-expression, the abandonment of important longings or aspirations.

2. Try to be more aware of the subtle sense of alarm when it arises, such as a tightening in your chest or face, a sinking feeling in your stomach, a sense of being off balance, or an increase in scanning or guardedness.

3. Then recognize that many alarm signals are actually not signals at all: they're just unpleasant *noise;* they're meaningless, like a car alarm that won't stop blapping.

Obviously, deal with real alarms. But, when it comes to the ones that are exaggerated or entirely bogus, don't react to these alarms with alarm.

4. Accept that bad things sometimes happen. There are always going to be uncertainties; people lose jobs, nice people get sick. We just have to live with the fact that we can't dodge all the bullets. When you come to terms with this, you stop trying to control—out of alarm—the things you can't.

Keep helping your body feel less alarmed. If it helps, you might imagine an inner iguana lodged in the most ancient and fearful structures of your brainstem—gently stroking its belly, soothing and settling it so it relaxes like a lizard on a warm rock. You could do the same with an inner rat, monkey, or caveman: continually softening and opening the body, breathing fully and letting go, sensing the strength and resolve you have inside.

Alarms may clang, but your awareness and intentions are much larger—like the sky dwarfing clouds. In effect, alarms and fears are held in a space of fearlessness. You see this zig-zaggy, up-and-down world clearly—and you are at peace with it. Try to return to this openhearted fearlessness again and again throughout your day.

2

NOTICE YOU'RE ALL RIGHT, RIGHT NOW

What to Know

To keep our ancestors alive, the brain evolved an ongoing internal trickle of unease. This little whisper of worry keeps you scanning your inner and outer worlds for signs of trouble. This background of unsettledness and watchfulness is so automatic that you can forget it's there. So see if you can tune in to a tension, guarding, or bracing in your body. Or a vigilance about your environment or other people. Or a block against *completely* relaxing, letting your guard down, letting go.

Try to sit at home for five minutes straight while feeling undefended, soft in your body, utterly comfortable in the moment as it is, at peace. This is impossible for most people.

The brain's default setting of apprehensiveness is a great way to keep a monkey looking over its shoulder for something about to pounce, but it's a crummy way to live. It wears down well-being, feeds anxiety and depression, and makes people turn away from the things that matter to them. And it's based on a lie.

In effect, that uneasiness in the background is continually whispering in your mental ear: *You're not safe, you're surrounded by threats, you can never afford to lower your guard.* But take a close look at *this* moment, right now. Probably, you are basically all right: no one is attacking you, you are not sick, no bombs are falling, there is no crisis where you sit. Things may be far from perfect, but you're okay.

Note that "right now" means *this* moment. When we go into the future, we worry and plan. When we go into the past, we resent and regret. Threads of fear are woven into the mental tapestries of past and future. Look again at the thin slice of time that is the *present.* In this moment: Are you basically okay? Is breathing okay? Is the heart beating? Is the mind working? The answers are almost certainly yes.

In daily life, it's possible to access this fundamental sense of all-rightness even while getting things done. You're not ignoring real threats or issues, or pretending that everything is perfect. It's not. But in the middle of everything, you can usually see that you're actually all right, right now.

What to Do

Several times a day, notice that you're basically all right. You may want more certainty or love, or simply ketchup for your French fries. Or you may want less pain, heartache, or national unemployment. All very reasonable. But meanwhile, underneath all the to-ing and fro-ing, you are okay. Underneath your desires and activities is an aliveness and an awareness that is doing fine this second.

There you are fixing dinner: notice that *I'm all right, right now*, and perhaps say that softly in your mind. Or you're driving: *I'm all right, right now.* Or you're talking with someone on a video call: *I'm all right, right now.*

Or doing emails or putting a child to bed: *I'm all right, right now.*

Notice that while feeling all right, right now, you can still get things done and deal with problems. The fear that bad things will happen if you let yourself feel okay is unfounded; let this sink in. You do not need to fear feeling all right!

Sometimes you're really *not* all right. Maybe something terrible has happened, or your body is very disturbed, or your mind is very upset. Do what you can at these times to ride out the storm. But as soon as possible, notice that the core of your being is okay, like the quiet place fifty feet underwater, beneath a hurricane howling above the sea.

Noticing that you're actually all right, right now is not laying a positive attitude over your life like a pretty veil. Instead, you are knowing a simple but profound fact: *In this moment I am all right.* You are sensing the truth in your body, deeper than fear, that it is breathing and living and okay. You are recognizing that your mind is functioning fine no matter how nutty and not-fine the contents swirling through it are.

Settling into this basic sense of okayness is a powerful way to build well-being and resources in your brain and being. You're taking a stand for the truth.

3

DIAPHRAGMATIC BREATHING

What to Know

A breathing exercise can be learned in a matter of minutes, and some of its benefits experienced immediately. Regular practice of a breathing exercise can have profound effects in a matter of weeks, if not days.

Choose a time and place to learn this diaphragmatic breathing exercise where you won't be disturbed. While you are learning to do this exercise, try to do your daily practice in the same place and at the same time. It's best to breathe through your nose unless otherwise instructed. If needed, clear your nasal passages before doing breathing exercises. If you can't clear them due to allergies or any other reason, it's okay to breathe through your mouth.

Take a moment to check in with yourself before beginning your breathing exercise. Take a second to notice how you're feeling throughout your body—from head to toe—doing your best to release points of obvious tension. If necessary, shift your position to be more comfortable.

At first, diaphragmatic breathing may feel awkward, especially if you typically breathe more shallowly through your chest. As a beginner, it can be useful to exaggerate the abdominal movement in this exercise, and to keep a hand on your abdomen as you breathe, in order to experience what diaphragmatic breathing feels like. Once you have this movement down, you don't need to exaggerate it, and you can place your hands at your sides. With practice, diaphragmatic breathing will feel more natural.

What to Do

1. Lie on your back and gently place one hand on your abdomen and one hand on your chest; follow your breathing. Notice how your

abdomen rises with each inhalation and falls with each exhalation. Alternatively, put a book on your abdomen, place your hands at your sides, and follow your breathing.

2. If you experience difficulty breathing into your abdomen, try one of the following:

• Exhale forcefully to empty your lungs. This will create a vacuum that will pull a deep breath into your abdomen. If you find yourself drifting back to shallow breaths from your chest, you may need to repeat this step.

• Press your hand down on your abdomen while you exhale, and then let your abdomen push your hand back up as you inhale deeply.

• Imagine that your abdomen is a balloon and that, as you inhale, you are filling it with air.

• Lie on your stomach with your head resting on your folded hands. Inhale deeply into your abdomen so you can feel your abdomen pushing against the floor.

3. Although most of the action is in your abdomen when you breathe diaphragmatically, your chest does move a little. Is your chest moving in harmony with your abdomen? Or is it rigid? As you inhale, first your abdomen, then your middle chest, and then your upper chest, will rise in one smooth movement. You might want to imagine filling a glass with water from the bottom to the top as you inhale.

4. Once you know what it feels like to breathe diaphragmatically, you can use this option to deepen and slow your breath even more. Smile slightly, inhale through your nose, and exhale through your mouth as though you are breathing out through a straw. Take long, slow, deep breaths that raise and lower your abdomen. Focus on the sound and feeling of your breathing as you become more and more relaxed.

5. When thoughts, feelings, and sensations catch your attention,

try to just notice them before returning to your breathing.

6. Practice diaphragmatic breathing for about five or ten minutes at a time, once or twice a day. Gradually extend the time you do this to twenty minutes.

7. At the end of each diaphragmatic-breathing session, take a little time to notice (and enjoy) how you feel.

8. Optional: You may want to check your body for tension at the beginning and end of each breathing practice session. Compare the level of tension you feel at the end of the exercise with the tension level you felt when you began.

4

CREATE YOUR SPECIAL PLACE

What to Know

We don't always have access to the places we love and that nourish us, but that doesn't mean you can't find respite by creating a special place in your mind that you can visit any time. In creating your special place, you will be making a mental refuge for relaxation and guidance. This place can be indoors or out. When structuring your place, follow these few guidelines:

- Allow a private entry into your place.
- Make it peaceful, comfortable, and safe.
- Fill your place with sensuous detail. Create a middle ground, foreground, and background.
- Allow room for an inner guide or other person to be there with you comfortably.

Make sure to use your imagination. Your special place might be at the end of a path that leads to a pond. Grass grows under your feet, the pond is about thirty yards away, and mountains are in the distance. You can feel the coolness of the air in this shady spot. The mockingbird is singing. The sun is bright on the pond. The honeysuckle's pungent smell attracts the bee buzzing over the flowers with their sweet nectar.

Or your special place might be a sparkling clean kitchen with cinnamon buns baking in the oven. Through the kitchen window you can see fields of yellow wheat. A window chime flutters in the breeze. At the table there's a cup of tea for your guest.

What to Do

Try recording this exercise and playing it back, or have a friend read it aloud to you slowly:

> To go to your safe place, lie down and be totally comfortable. Close your eyes ... Walk slowly to a quiet place in your mind ... Your place can be inside or outside ... It

needs to be peaceful and safe ... Picture yourself unloading your anxieties, your worries ... Notice the view in the distance ... What do you smell? What do you hear? Notice what is before you ... Reach out and touch it ... How does it feel? Smell it ... Hear it ... Make the temperature comfortable ... Be safe here ... Look around for a special spot, a private spot ... Find the path to this place ... Feel the ground with your feet ... Look above you ... What do you see? Hear? Smell? Walk down this path until you can enter your own quiet, comfortable, safe place.

You have arrived at your special place ... What is under your feet? How does it feel? Take several steps ... What do you see above you? What do you hear? Do you hear something else? Reach for and touch something ... What is its texture? Are there pens, paper, or paints nearby? Is there sand to draw in, or clay to work? Go to them, handle them, smell them. These are your special tools, tools *for your inner guide to reveal ideas or feelings to you ... Look as far as you can see ... What do you see? What do you hear? What aromas do you notice?*

Sit or lie in your special place ... Notice its smells, sounds, sights ... This is your place, and nothing can harm you here ... If danger is here, expel it ... Spend three to five minutes realizing you are relaxed, safe, and comfortable.

Memorize this place's smells, tastes, sights, sounds ... You can come back and relax here whenever you want ... Leave by the same path or entrance ... Notice the ground, touch things near you ... Look far away and appreciate the view ... Remind yourself that this special place you created can be entered whenever you wish. Say an affirmation such as "can relax here" or "This is my special place. I can come here whenever I wish."

Now open your eyes and spend a few seconds appreciating your relaxation.

5

TAKE REFUGE

What to Know

All across the world there exist places of refuge. People fleeing for their lives during times of instability can come to these places and be sheltered. For example, in medieval Europe a person could take refuge in a church and be protected there.

Less formally, we all need everyday refuges from challenges, sorrows, and the sheer craziness of the world. Otherwise, you get too exposed to the cold winds of life, or just too drained by the daily grind. After a while without refuge, you can feel like you're running on empty. And refuge is more than just a place. It can include people, memories, ideas—anyone or anything that provides reliable sanctuary and protection when you need it. Refuge can be found in anyone or anything that's reassuring, comforting, and supportive. Wherever you feel as though you can let down your guard to gather strength and wisdom, there is refuge.

A refuge could be a form of self-care, such as curling up in bed with a good book, having a meal with friends, or making a To Do list to organize your day. Or it could more simple, such as remembering your grandmother, appreciating the feeling of strength in your body, trusting the findings of science, or talking with a trusted friend. Many religions also offer refuges—sacred settings, texts, individuals, teachings, rituals, objects, and congregations.

Your refuge might also be *practice* itself: the pursuit of a habit, skill, or ritual each day. Perhaps it's shaving a minute off of a daily run, or perhaps it's a meditation practice. Either way, some feel most in their refuge while pursuing a practice as fully as they can. It makes them feel good to trust that if they keep plugging away, then they can gradually become happier and more loving. What gives you a sense of refuge?

What to Do

Make a written or mental list of at least a few things that are refuges for you. It can be a breakthrough to imagine that many refuges already exist inside you, that you can live *from* them as an expression *of* them in this life. When you take refuge in this way, you are giving yourself over to wholesome forces, and letting them work through you, carrying you along.

You may take refuge explicitly, with words, by saying things in your mind like *I take refuge in_____. Or I abide as_____. Or _____ flows through me.* Or just sense the refuge without words. Feel what it is like for you to be in it, safe and supported, *home.*

Try to do this every day, as soon as you remember to do so. It only takes a few minutes or less. And you can even do it in the middle of traffic or a meeting. Once you have finished taking refuge, sense the good feelings and thoughts sinking deeply into you, filling you up, and weaving themselves into your being—a resource and inner light that you'll take with you wherever you go.

6

PROGRESSIVE RELAXATION

What to Know

Progressive relaxation can be practiced lying down or seated in a chair. Each muscle group is tensed from five to seven seconds and then released and relaxed for twenty to thirty seconds. These lengths of time are simply rules of thumb and don't have to be rigorously adhered to. This procedure is repeated at least once. If a particular muscle is difficult to relax, you can practice tensing and releasing it up to five times.

Once the procedure is familiar enough to be remembered, keep your eyes closed and focus your attention on just one muscle group at a time.

It might be easier if you make a recording of the basic procedure to facilitate your relaxation program. Remember to pause long enough for tensing and relaxing each muscle or muscle group before going on to the next muscle or muscle group. Be extra cautious when tensing your neck and back, as excessive tightening can result in muscle or spinal damage. Also, overtightening your toes or feet can result in muscle cramping, so be gentle with yourself. Trust the feelings in your body and let relaxation in.

What to Do

In this exercise, whole muscle groups are simultaneously tensed and then relaxed. People new to this technique sometimes make the error of relaxing tension gradually. This slow-motion release of tension may look relaxed, but it actually requires sustained tension. When you release the tension in a particular muscle, let it go instantly; let your muscles become suddenly limp.

This practice is best performed sitting in a chair, tensing each muscle group from five to seven seconds and then relaxing from fifteen to thirty seconds. Remember to notice the contrast between the sensations of tension and relaxation.

1. Curl both fists, tightening your biceps and forearms. Relax.
2. Roll your head around on your neck clockwise in a complete circle, then reverse. Relax.
3. Wrinkle up the muscles of your face like a walnut: forehead wrinkled, eyes squinted, mouth opened, and shoulders hunched. Relax.
4. Arch your shoulders back as you take a deep breath into your chest. Hold. Relax. Take a deep breath, pushing out your stomach. Hold. Relax.
5. Straighten your legs and point your toes back toward your face, tightening your shins. Hold. Relax. Straighten your legs and curl your toes, simultaneously tightening your calves, thighs, and buttocks. Relax.

Although initially you should start the progressive relaxation in a quiet place, with practice, you can use it anytime during the day when you notice you are tense.

7

SITTING MEDITATION

What to Know

Generally speaking, any amount of time spent meditating is more relaxing than not meditating at all. When you first begin to practice meditation, maintain the meditation for only as long as is comfortable, even if this is just for five minutes a day. If you feel that you are forcing yourself to sit, you may develop an aversion to practicing meditation at all. As you progress and meditation becomes easier, you will find yourself wanting to extend your time. In terms of relaxation, practicing for twenty to thirty minutes once a day is sufficient, though you'll notice benefits with even less.

What to Do

The simplest way to begin meditation is by focusing on your breath.

1. Choose a comfortable sitting posture.
2. Take three large breaths from your belly and then relax your breathing back to normal. You can close your eyes if you like, but it is not required.
3. Bring your attention to the gentle rise and fall of your breath. Like ocean waves coming in to the shore and going out, your breath is always there. You can focus on your inhale and exhale, the sensations of your breath entering your nose or mouth, or the sensations of your breath filling your lungs and diaphragm.
4. Whenever your mind wanders, gently bring your attention back to focus on your breath. Let your breath be your anchor to this present moment.

5. When you find yourself becoming distracted by thoughts, simply notice and acknowledge them.

6. One way to work with thoughts is to name them as you notice them. If you notice you are worrying, silently say to yourself, *Worry, worry, there is worry.* You can call it "planning," "reminiscing," "longing," "thinking," or whatever it is in just the same way—label it and move on. This will help you to stop identifying with your thoughts and learn how to let go in to create more spaciousness and inner peace.

This meditation can take between ten and thirty minutes to do. With practice, you will become able to rest your attention on your breath more effortlessly and to let go of your thoughts more easily.

8

RAPID RELAXATION

What to Know

Rapid relaxation can bring the time you need to relax down to about thirty seconds. Being able to relax that quickly can bring real relief during stressful situations. It's a good idea to practice rapid relaxation many times a day as you move through different activities and states of mind.

In rapid relaxation, you will pick a special relaxation cue. Choose something that you see regularly throughout the day, such as your watch, a certain clock, or the picture you pass as you walk down the hall to the bathroom. If you can, mark that special cue with a piece of colored tape while you're practicing this technique.

What to Do

When you're ready to begin, look at your special cue. Breathe in and relax.

Then breathe in and relax again. Continue to look at your cue and think *relax.* Breathe in and relax. You are breathing deeply and evenly, and you continue to think *relax* each time you exhale. Let the relaxation spread throughout your body. Try to notice any tension in your body, and send relaxation, as much as possible, to every muscle that isn't needed for whatever activity you are currently doing.

Every time you look at your cue throughout the day, go through these three simple steps:

1. Take two or three deep, even breaths, exhaling slowly through your mouth.
2. Think *relax* each time you exhale, as you continue to breathe deeply.
3. Scan your body for any tension. Focus on those muscles that need to relax and empty them of tension.

More to Do

Try to use your relaxation cue fifteen times a day to relax quickly in natural, non-stressful situations. This will instill the habit of checking yourself for tension and moving back to a state of deep relaxation throughout the day. After your first few days of practice, you may want to change the color of the tape on your relaxation cue—or even change the cue altogether. This will keep the idea of relaxation fresh in your mind. Finally, see if you can use rapid relaxation to calm yourself during one or two particularly stressful moments of the day.

9

RELAXING VISUALIZATION

What to Know

Using imagery, or visualization, is another beneficial relaxation strategy. Some people have the ability to imagine themselves in another location, and can use visualization to effectively attain a relaxed state. If this sounds familiar (for instance, from what you practiced in exercise 4, "Create Your Special Place," you may find that imagining yourself on a beach or in a peaceful forest glade allows you to achieve a more satisfying state of relaxation than does muscle relaxation. The truth is, it doesn't matter whether you attain this state by directly focusing on your breathing and muscles, or by imagining yourself in a setting that allows you to relax. Whatever form of relaxation you prefer, the most important goal is to achieve *deep breathing* and *relaxed muscles.* That's the key to reducing activation that constant anxious thinking leaves you with.

What to Do

Read through the following description of a relaxing situation, then take a few moments to close your eyes and imagine yourself in that setting.

Imagine yourself on a warm beach. Feel the sun warming your skin and the cool breeze coming off the water. Listen to the sounds of the waves as they wash against the shore and the calls of birds in the distance. Allow yourself to relax and enjoy the beach for several minutes.

How well were you able to imagine yourself in the described setting? If the visualization arose for you readily and you find it pleasant and engaging, we highly recommend that you use imagery as one of your relaxation strategies. It may allow you to achieve a relaxed state more effectively than other approaches. On the other hand, if you found it difficult to relax using this method and noticed your mind wandering, you'll probably find other strategies more helpful.

More to Do

When you use imagery to relax, you take yourself to another location in your imagination. Start by slowing your breathing and relaxing your body as you mentally travel to another scene. We've provided a guided script, based on the image of a beach, to give you an overview of the process, but feel free to choose any location you enjoy. The key is to close your eyes and allow yourself to experience this special place in detail. Try to use all of your senses (sight, sound, smell, touch, and even taste) as you imagine yourself in this particularly relaxing situation. You might ask someone to read this script to you so you can close your eyes and focus.

Imagine yourself walking on a sandy path to a beach. As you walk on the path, you're surrounded by trees that keep you in dark shade. You feel the sand begin to get into your shoes as you walk along. You can hear the leaves in the trees softly moving in the wind, but up ahead you hear another sound: gentle waves washing up on shore.

As you continue, you leave the shade of the trees to walk out onto a sunny, sandy beach. The sun warms your head and shoulders as you stand still for a moment to take in your surroundings. The sky is a beautiful shade of blue, and wispy white clouds seem to hang motionless in the sky. You take off your shoes and feel the warm sand as your feet sink in. Holding your shoes, you move toward the water. The sound of the waves rhythmically washing up on the shore has a hypnotic quality. You breathe deeply, in unison with the waves.

The water is dark blue, and far off on the horizon you can see a darker blue line where the water meets the light blue sky. In the distance, you see two sailboats, one with a white sail and one with a red sail; they appear to be racing one other. The damp smell of *driftwood reaches your nose, and you see some driftwood nearby. You place your shoes on a smooth, weathered log and walk toward the waves.*

Seagulls swoop overhead, and you hear their excited cries as they glide on the gentle breeze coming in with the waves. You feel the breeze on your skin and smell its freshness. As you walk toward the waves, you see the sun reflected on the water. You walk into the damp sand, leaving footprints now as you walk along the shore. A wave breaks over your feet, surprisingly cold at first.

You stand still as the waves wash over your ankles. Listening to the repetitive sound of the waves and the cries of the gulls, you feel the wind blowing your hair away from your face. You take slow, deep breaths of the cool, clean air...

We recommend that you end each imagery session gradually, counting backward slowly from ten to one. With each number, gradually become more aware of your surroundings—the actual environment around you. When you reach one, open your eyes and return to the present moment feeling refreshed and relaxed.

Through imagery, you can take a trip each day that's limited only by your imagination and that can decrease your stress in just a few minutes. Choose locations that you can explore and that lead to feelings of peace and comfort. As you practice, remember that visualization will be most effective at reducing overwhelm if you achieve relaxation in your muscles, and slow and deepen your breathing.

10

FEEL SAFER

What to Know

Consider these two mistakes:

1. You think there's a tiger in the bushes, but actually there isn't one.
2. You think there's no tiger in the bushes, but actually one is about to pounce.

Most of us make the first mistake much more often than the second one, for several reasons:

1. Evolution has given us an anxious brain. In order to survive and pass on genes, it's better to make the first mistake a thousand times rather than make the second mistake even once; the cost of the first mistake is fear for no reason, but the cost of the second mistake could be death.
2. This general tendency in the human brain is exacerbated by temperament—some people are

naturally more anxious than others—and by life experiences (such as growing up in a dangerous neighborhood or experiencing trauma).

3. When you're saturated with media, news about outbreaks, disasters, economic turmoil, and horrible things happening to other people sifts into your mind—even though your own local situation is probably much less dangerous.

4. In ways that have been repeated throughout history, political groups try to gain or hold onto power by exaggerating apparent threats.

Most of us have a kind of paper tiger paranoia. It's definitely important to recognize the real tigers in life, which come in many shapes and sizes: maybe it's an impending layoff at work, a cough that won't go away, a friend who keeps letting you down, or the health risks of returning to "normal" after a serious public health outbreak. However, it's also important to try to recognize the ways that you—like most people—routinely overestimate threats while underestimating the resources inside and around you.

Most of us also feel much less safe than we actually are even during times of distress. The unfortunate results of this include unpleasant feelings of worry and anxiety; stress-related illnesses; less capacity to be patient or generous with others; and a greater tendency to be snippy or angry (the engine of most aggression is fear). It doesn't feel good to stay stuck on Threat Level Orange, does it?

As hard times remind us, there is no perfect safety in this life. Each of us will face disease, old age, and death—as well as many other lesser but still painful experiences. And many of us must deal with unsafe conditions in the community, workplace, or home. This said, consider in your heart of hearts whether you deserve to feel safer than you do: whether you are more braced against life, more guarded, more cautious, more anxious, more frozen, more appeasing, more rigid, or more prickly than you truly need to be.

By guarding yourself against paper tigers, you can better prepare yourself for the rare but inevitable times when a real tiger lurks behind the bushes.

What to Do

Here are some ways to help yourself feel safer. Do these, and a growing internal sense of calm and confidence will emerge to match the reality of the people and places around you:

- Bring to mind the sense of being with someone who cares about you.
- Recall a time you felt strong.
- Recognize that you are in a protected setting.
- Mentally list some of the resources inside and around you that you could draw on to deal with what life throws you.
- Take a few breaths, with l-o-n-g exhalations, and relax.
- All the while, keep helping yourself feel safer; more sheltered, supported, and capable; and less vigilant, tense, or fearful.
- Become more aware of what it's like to feel safer, and let those good feelings sink in so you can remember them in your body and

find your way back to them in the future.

You can practice with the methods above in many ways, such as first thing in the morning (plus several times later on in the day if you tend to be fearful). Also try them in specific unsettling situations like before speaking up in a meeting, driving in traffic, getting on an airplane, or working through a sticky issue with your partner. The more often you remind yourself of all the ways that you are safe, the safer you will feel on a daily basis.

PART II

FACING WORRY AND ANXIETY

11

CHANGE YOUR INTERPRETATIONS

What to Know

When you experience a situation or event, the situation or event itself doesn't cause you to have an emotion. If you doubt this, consider that different people have different emotional reactions to the same event. Therefore, the event itself can't be the cause of the emotion.

By being aware of your interpretations during stressful situations and considering how you might change them, you can take charge of the emotional reactions in your brain. Keep in mind that changing your interpretations won't always be easy, because those interpretations are often shaped by your past experiences and expectations. There are also some emotional reactions that you find useful and want to keep.

However, just knowing that you have the ability to alter your brain's interpretations can go a long way toward reducing your anxiety. It'll take some work to think through a situation and identify the way you want to interpret it, but once you do, getting a handle on your anxiety can be as easy as remembering three simple words: *event→interpretation→emotion.*

What to Do

On a piece of paper, list several situations in which you feel anxiety. Then, for each, see if you can identify the interpretations that lead you to react in an anxious manner.

Next, spend some time brainstorming alternative interpretations for each anxiety-igniting interpretation you identified. If you play with this a bit, you can probably see how different interpretations could lead to a wide range of emotional responses. Of course, for the purposes of reducing anxiety, you'd want to focus on interpretations that lead to a more calm, balanced state of mind.

Once you've identified alternative interpretations, we recommend that you say them out loud in order to establish them more fully. This will strengthen your ability to modify your interpretation. In the beginning, the process of changing interpretations may feel awkward; you may not find your new interpretations convincing. But with time, you'll find that these thoughts become stronger and arise on their own more often.

The more you deliberately use them, the more they'll become a part of your habitual way of responding. Changing the way you think isn't easy, but if you devote some attention to noticing your interpretations and are dedicated to looking at situations differently, you can do it.

12

TAKE YOUR WORRIES FOR A WALK

What to Know

If you have dogs, you generally need to take those dogs for a walk, unless you have room to let them run. There will be times when you don't feel like it—when it's cold and snowy outside, when you're wrapped up in working from home, or when you have a headache, and you just don't feel like doing it. But if you don't let those dogs poop and pee outdoors, pretty soon they'll do it indoors. That won't do much for your headache or your work! Even when you take those dogs for a walk, they don't always do what you want. Sometimes they race ahead, trying to pull you along. Sometimes they lag behind, and you have to make them follow. Sometimes they try to eat stuff they shouldn't, or bark at your neighbors.

Those dogs are a lot like your worrisome thoughts. Sometimes they demand attention when you really don't feel like giving it, and sometimes they just don't do things the way you wish they would. But life is better with the walks than without them!

You've probably noticed that you tend to worry less when you're busy and more when you're idle. Episodes of chronic worry tend to fade faster when you're active because your brain has more exciting things to focus on. We're not saying that the solution is simply make yourself busy. Unfortunately, that's too much like trying to get rid of the thoughts. Not that there's anything terribly wrong with getting rid of the thoughts, if it can be done simply and effectively. It's just that trying directly to get rid of the thoughts usually just ends up making them more persistent and plentiful.

So it is with worries. Life is a come-as-you-are party, and you can't control whether worry comes on a lazy Wednesday evening or the night of a big party. You can, however, control what you do about it.

Would you be happier without the worries? Yes, but that choice isn't immediately available. Would you be better off lying in bed, alone with your worries? Probably not!

What to Do

Pack up your worries and bring them with you. Go on about your business—the worries may leave sooner that way. And if they don't, at least you're participating in life while you wait for them to pass. It's as simple as that.

When they're worried, people often object to the idea of getting involved with a project of any kind, on the grounds that they will be able to do a better job when they're not worried so much. Similarly, they often want to isolate themselves from others out of a concern that others will notice their distress and be bothered by it.

Both are instances of how our gut instincts of how to handle worry tend to be the opposite of what would actually be helpful. Often, our instincts will tell us that we need, first, to get rid of the worrisome thoughts we're experiencing, and then, afterwards, to get involved with activities outside our skin.

But it's really the other way around. Your involvement with the world around you will tend to direct your energy and attention there—and leave less of it in your head. Moreover, when you interact with the external world, you get more involved with realistic rules about how things actually work. When you're in your head, by contrast, you can imagine anything. This is why our worries about the future are almost always worse than anything that actually happens in real life—because there are no rules in your head, anything seems possible!

13

REPLACE THOUGHTS

What to Know

Studies have shown that trying to erase or silence a thought simply isn't an effective approach. For example, if you're asked to not think about pink elephants, the image of pink elephants will, of course, leap into your mind even if you haven't been thinking about pink elephants all day. And the harder you try to stop thinking about pink elephants, the more you think of them. If you have a tendency toward obsession, you're probably familiar with this pattern. Erasing a thought by constantly reminding yourself not to think about it (and therefore thinking about it) activates the circuitry storing that thought and makes it stronger.

You might be successful in interrupting a thought by specifically telling yourself "Stop!" This technique is called *thought stopping*. However, the next step is crucial. If you *replace* the thought you stopped with a different thought, it's more likely that you'll keep the first thought out of your mind.

What to Do

Let's say you're working in your garden and keep worrying that at any moment you'll encounter a snake. Tell yourself "Stop!" and then begin thinking about something else: a song on the radio, the names of the flowers you intend to plant in your garden, ideas you have for a loved one's birthday present—basically anything captivating and, ideally, pleasant. By replacing the anxiety-provoking thought with something else that engages your mind, you'll make it more likely that you won't return to that thought.

Therefore, *Don't erase—replace!* is the best approach with anxiety-igniting thoughts. If you notice that you're thinking something like, *I can't handle this,* focus on replacing that thought with a coping thought, such as *This isn't easy, but I will get through it.* By repeating this coping thought to yourself, you'll teach your brain that it can think in more adaptive, flexible ways, and activate circuitry that will protect you from anxiety in the future. It takes some practice, but your new thoughts will eventually become habitual.

14

MAKE A WORRY APPOINTMENT

What to Know

A worry appointment is time you set aside exclusively for worry. This idea may seem strange to you because it runs counter to our usual instincts. But that's often how it seems when you fight fire with fire. Fighting fire with fire isn't just a metaphor. It's a technique used to control forest fires. It involves deliberately burning all the flammable material that would otherwise fuel the fire in its spread. When the forest fire arrives at the burned-out part, it falters because it has no fuel left to keep it burning.

Resistance is the fuel by which chronic worry spreads. Watching yourself worry may sound like a bizarre, unwelcome exercise, but it works. And the most immediate benefit of a worry appointment is the ability to postpone worry. Many people find that this enables them to sweep large portions of their day relatively clear of worry. However, it only works if you actually do the worry periods as prescribed. If you try to postpone worries, knowing that you probably won't actually show up for the worry appointments, the postponing probably won't work for you. So don't try to fool yourself!

Postponing worry would probably be sufficient reason for most of us to justify making (and keeping) a worry appointment. But there's more! Over time, worry appointments can also help change your automatic responses to worry, and help you take the content of the worrisome thoughts less seriously. How about trying it now?

What to Do

During a worry appointment, which will last about ten minutes, you'll engage in pure worry. Devote your full attention to worrying and nothing else. Don't engage in other activities like driving, showering, eating, cleaning, texting, listening to music, riding on a train, and so on. Spend the full ten minutes indulging in pure unadulterated worry.

You might even make a list of worries ahead of time to make sure you don't run out of things to worry about. Remember, don't try to solve problems, reassure yourself, minimize problems, relax, clear your mind, reason with yourself, or take any other steps to stop worrying. Simply worry, which for most of us means reciting a lot of "what if" questions about scary possibilities over and over again.

Be sure to schedule your worry appointments in advance. Pick times when you have privacy and don't have to answer the phone or the doorbell, talk to others, look after the dog or the kids, and so on. Worry appointments will probably seem strange and awkward at first. However, if you're reading this book, you'll likely have lots of experience with worrying. Here's a chance to use that experience for your benefit!

More to Do

One more idea: worry out loud, ideally in front of a mirror. This probably sounds like a strange suggestion, but don't skip it. It's important! The advantage of worrying this way is that it helps you become a better *observer* of your worry.

Most worry is subliminal. It occurs when we're multitasking. We worry while driving, attending video calls, showering, eating, watching television, or doing some routine work that doesn't demand much attention. And since we rarely give worry our full attention, it's easy for it to continue endlessly. Because worry comes in the form of our own subliminal thoughts, it has more power to influence us. And we all tend to assume that *If it's my thought, there must be something to it.* We tend not to notice that we can think all kinds of nonsense, that thoughts are often only anxiety symptoms, nothing more.

When you worry out loud, you don't just say the worries, you hear them. When you worry in front of a mirror, you see yourself doing the worrying.

You're not just worrying in the back of your mind. You're hearing and watching yourself as you worry. The worry is no longer subliminal, and this will probably help you get a better perspective on it. Worry appointments are deliberately structured this way to convert worry from a multitasking activity to a unitary one in which you only do one thing—worry—and you do it with the fullest awareness and attention possible.

15

CHANGE THE ANXIETY CHANNEL

What to Know

Some people have a strong tendency to use the brain in ways that create anxiety. They are often quite talented at imagining dreadful events or coming up with negative scenarios. In fact, people who are highly creative and imaginative are sometimes more prone to anxiety for this very reason. The way they think about their life and imagine events frequently captures the attention of the brain and provokes a reaction. People who catastrophize are typical examples.

If this is an issue for you, think of your brain as cable television. Despite having hundreds of channels to choose from, you get stuck on the Anxiety Channel. Unfortunately, it appears to be your favorite. You may focus on thoughts and images that have anxiety-igniting potential without realizing it. Or perhaps you're aware of this focus but argue with the thoughts, just as you might argue with televised political commentators you don't agree with. Arguing with your thoughts is similar. You don't want to spend too much time arguing with your thoughts because that tends to keep the focus on them and maintain the circuitry underlying them.

What to Do

There are many ways to change the channel. One way is through *distraction:* moving your focus of attention to something completely different. Distraction can be a very effective way to manage anxiety. For example, instead of thinking about the stress of business openings after a lockdown, change the channel and focus on a different topic. You could focus on having a conversation with someone, coming up with menus for the week, or playing with your kids or a pet. Distracting yourself by focusing on other activities or ideas is one of the simplest ways to change the channel.

One of the best kinds of distraction is play. So many anxious people are gripped by an excruciating seriousness and therefore have difficulty loosening up and having fun. Cultivating a sense of playfulness is essential. And it isn't necessary to wait until you aren't anxious to become playful. Be playful to find relief. Playing games, joking, and engaging in silliness are some of the best distractions. Humor is essential in coping with life's challenges.

Using distraction to change the channel can immediately reduce anxiety in a given situation. Beyond that, the more you deliberately direct your attention to other topics when you notice you're focused on anxiety-igniting thoughts, the more you increase activity in new circuits and reduce activity in circuits focused on anxiety-producing topics or images. The circuitry that you use the most becomes the strongest, and circuitry you don't use becomes weaker and less likely to be activated. So you don't just reduce your anxiety for a few moments; you rewire your brain.

16

PUT YOUR WORRIES IN A LINEUP

What to Know

This is what you would do if you had been the victim of a crime, like a mugging or a robbery: You'd report it to the police, and they would ask you to sit down with the police artist and describe the mugger so the artist could draw him. This would help the police apprehend the perpetrator. It wouldn't be pleasant, but it would be worth doing. Sketching out some of your worries to do this review might be your first step toward changing your relationship with worry for the better. Is it worth a try?

What to Do

What are some worries that bothered you recently? Write down a few of them on your phone, or do it the old-fashioned way with pen and paper. Next, take a look at the worries you wrote down, and apply this two-part test.

1. Is there a problem that exists now in the external world around you?
2. If there is, can you do something to change it now?

If you answered yes to both questions, then perhaps you should put this book aside and go do something to change the problem now. If there's a significant problem now, in the physical world you inhabit, and you can do something to change it, go ahead and do that!

On the other hand, if you answered no to both (or yes to the first question and no to the second), then you're dealing with chronic worry. You're nervous, and that worrisome thought is just a symptom of being nervous. Maybe your answer was neither yes nor no but included thoughts like these:

- *It's not happening right now, but what if it starts soon?*
- *If I don't stay on guard and watch out, bad things might happen.*

- *I hope it doesn't happen, but how can I be sure?*
- *It probably won't happen, but it would be so awful if it did...*
- *Isn't it possible that this might happen? I sure hope it doesn't!*
- *If I don't worry about it, then it probably will happen.*

Thoughts like these are particularly tricky. You're likely to have such thoughts when you try to persuade yourself that some dreaded event just isn't possible, that it won't and can't happen. It's very difficult to prove a negative, to prove that something won't happen in the future; trying to do so is a losing game, a response that brings you more worry rather than less.

17

DO THE OPPOSITE

What to Know

What's good for danger? Three things: fight, flight, and freeze. If it looks weaker than me, I'll fight. If it looks slower than me, I'll run. And if it looks stronger and faster than me, I'll freeze, hoping it doesn't see so well. That's all we have for danger.

When you experience doubt, worry, and anxiety, your brain treats it like danger. Except our gut instinct of how to respond to unwanted, chronic worry is pretty much dead wrong. You can't fight, run from, or freeze and hope worry doesn't see you. In fact, you are usually better off doing the opposite of your gut instinct.

Fight, flight, and freeze methods all involve opposing the worry—fighting to stop worrying or to distract yourself; running from worry by repeatedly seeking reassurance from friends, a partner, or the internet; or freezing in the face of worry by numbing out with drugs or alcohol. Worry and anxious feelings, however, aren't real danger. They're more like plain old discomfort. And what's good for discomfort? A million variations on "chill out and let it pass." Let's look at some below.

What to Do

What's good for danger is the opposite of what's good for discomfort, so make no effort. Simply allow the environment to support you, and go on with your business.

When you treat worry as a danger that must be stopped or avoided, it's as if your compass is off by 180 degrees, showing north when you're facing south. If you have a compass that's off by 180 degrees, you can still find your way home as long as you remember that you need to go in the opposite direction it suggests. Your gut instinct of how to handle worry has probably been to take its content seriously, opposing it and seeking to avoid it. We need something very different for the discomfort and doubt of worry.

This way would allow us to recognize the doubts and uncertainties that occur to us, and also allow for the way our brains may be overly vigilant in imagining future dangers. It would allow us to distinguish between thoughts that occur in our brains (our internal world) and events that occur (or don't) in the external world. And it would allow us to live more comfortably with the reality that we don't control our thoughts, and that our thoughts are not always our best guide to what is happening, or will be happening, in our external world.

18

COUNT YOUR WORRIES

What to Know

Many people try very hard to distract themselves from their worrisome thoughts. If distraction really worked, you probably wouldn't be reading this book. You would have already dismissed and banished your unwanted worries with some pleasant distraction or another. Unfortunately, worries don't work that way; it's actually quite the opposite. The more you try to eject thoughts from your mind, the more they keep coming back in—kind of like unwanted drunks at a party.

That doesn't mean the effort to distract yourself is worthless, however. It can point to some useful information. Consider this question: When you are motivated to distract yourself from a problem, what does it tell you about that problem? Think about that for a minute. What kind of problems do we usually want to distract ourselves from?

Imagine that you were standing in line at a bank when a robbery broke out and you heard gunshots. How likely would you be to take out your checkbook and balance it in order to distract yourself from the unpleasant gunplay? Probably not very likely! You'd be too busy diving to the floor or looking for some cover or an exit. You'd be trying to protect yourself, not distract yourself.

The reality is that we're motivated to distract ourselves from unpleasant and worrisome thoughts when we're not facing a clear and present danger. When the chips are not down. When the babbling of our thinking, rather than the automatic self-defense responses to real danger, is center stage.

What to Do

Get yourself some bottles of Tic Tacs, or any kind of mint that comes in fixed quantities. Tic Tacs, for instance, come in bottles of sixty and one hundred (except in Australia, where they come in bottles of fifty—go figure!), but any kind of mint or candy that comes in a fixed number per bottle will do. Keep it with you at all times, in your pocket, purse, or briefcase.

Whenever you notice a "what if" thought, take out your bottle of Tic Tacs and remove one: you can eat it, flick it onto the street, or toss it in the garbage. Whatever you do with it is fine—just remove one from the bottle and close the lid.

You can use this as a way to track the number of times you experience a "what if" thought during the week. If you prefer, you could use some other method, like a clicker. The Tic Tac method works well, though, because it is more likely to interrupt you in your mental business as usual. And, if you feel self-conscious about doing this kind of self-monitoring, no one will notice a thing—just a person eating a mint!

One more thing before you start. As you start using the Tic Tacs, you might be displeased when you notice how many times you catch yourself in the act of "what if"-ing. You might feel overwhelmed when you realize how often this thought occurs to you. You might feel, initially, that you would have much preferred that we hadn't ever brought it to your attention.

Don't be fooled. This is the good news because you've been having all those thoughts for some time, long before you started this book. The only thing that's different now is that you're noticing them and keeping track of your counts for a couple of weeks to help you really get into this habit of passively observing "what if" instead of getting caught up in worry cycles.

When you notice that you feel the urge to distract yourself, this can be a powerful reminder of what the game is. The chips are not down, you are not in danger, and that's why you are motivated to distract. If you actually *were* under the gun, you wouldn't even think of distraction!

19

HUMOR YOUR WORRY

What to Know

Worry is counterintuitive. When you try to remove it, it only becomes more persistent. Instead of removing worry, try to think of your goal as being to get better at hearing and accepting worry for what it is—simply a thought, a twitch in your internal world. It's okay to have thoughts—smart ones, dumb ones, pleasant ones, angry ones, scary ones, and so on. We don't have that much choice in the matter. We all have lots of thoughts. And a lot of them are misleading and exaggerated.

People with chronic worry go through a cycle. When they have a time of extra worry, they label it "a bad time" and struggle to bring it to an end. When they have a time of reduced worry, they label it "a good time" and try to keep the worry at bay. They're always trying to adjust their menu of thoughts to manage their worry—and it usually brings a very different result than they intended.

What's a person to do? When you try to get rid of the "bad times," it often prolongs and strengthens them. When you try to hold on to the "good times," they get ripped from your hands. Frustrating, right?

Let's recall that important observation: *The harder I try, the worse it gets.* How can you apply that here? You might identify your worry thought and keep that thought in mind. What does that mean, to keep that thought in mind? It means the opposite of what you do when you try to keep that thought out of mind! You deliberately keep the thought at hand, playing with it, repeating it, trying not to forget about it, maybe checking in with yourself every three minutes or so to make sure you remember to repeat the thought to yourself periodically. Why would anyone do that? Well, if it's true that *the harder I try, the worse it gets,* you'll probably get better results doing the opposite of what you usually do!

What to Do

Simply take the thought, accept it, and exaggerate it. There's a training exercise in improvisational theater called "Yes, and..." In this exercise, you accept whatever the other person in the scene has just told you, and build on it by adding something else. You don't disagree, contradict, or deny what the other player just said. You accept it and add to it. This is probably the most fundamental rule of improvisational comedy—no denial! Instead, accept whatever the other performers offer you and build on it.

This rule works on stage and will also work in your own mind. Here are some examples of humoring the thoughts in this way:

What if I freak out in the grocery store and they have to restrain me?

- *Yes, and then the checkout clerk will have everyone probably parade me through town before taking me to the asylum, and I'll be on the nightly news for everyone to see.*

- *What if I get so nervous on my video call that my hands shake so everyone can see?*
- *Yes, and I'll probably spill hot soup all over my laptop and cause second degree burns, not to mention that my computer will be ruined, and I will probably be fired.*
- *What if I get a fatal illness?*
- *Yes, and I better call the hospital to make a reservation now, and probably the funeral home, too.*

The point of this response is not to get rid of the worry. Instead, the point is to become more accepting of the worry so that it matters less to you. It's to get better at hearing and accepting the thought for what it is—simply a thought, a twitch in your internal world.

20

THE WORRY EXPERIMENT

What to Know

Your automatic thoughts are like an unending soundtrack that accompanies you your entire life. Sometimes the thoughts are relevant, sometimes not; sometimes pleasant, sometimes not; sometimes accurate, sometimes not. There's no off switch, no volume control. We live in our thoughts the same way a goldfish lives in water.

Neither you nor I get to pick our thoughts. We can, however, pick how we respond to them, and we can certainly pick what we do with our time on this planet. We don't need to get our thoughts arranged the way we might like in order to do things we want to do.

When people try to hold on to good thoughts and get rid of the bad thoughts—where do they do it? In their heads! As the activity of life goes on around them, they're missing out, because they're inside, trying once again to rearrange the furniture, rather than coming out into the sunlight where life actually occurs. If ever feel that you're missing out on life because of worry, try to let your thoughts come and go in your head while you tend to what's important to you out in the world, the environment of people, places, and objects that you live in.

What to Do

Step One. Create a sentence, twenty-five words maximum, that expresses the strongest version you can create of one of your typical worries, something that's been bothering you recently. The first two words will probably be "what if," so you really only have twenty-three words to play with. Try to create a thought that not only includes the terrible event you fear but also incorporates the long-term consequences of this problem, the angst you'll feel in your old age as you remember this bad event, and so on. Below are two examples.

1. For someone who worries about losing his/her sanity:

WEAK: *What if I go crazy?*

BETTER: *What if I go crazy and end up in an institution?*

GOOD: *What if I go crazy, end up in an institution, and live a long, miserable, pointless life—forgotten, toothless, with bad hair, abandoned and alone?*

2. For someone who worries about looking foolish in front of people:

WEAK: *What if I get really nervous during the conference call?*

BETTER: *What if I get really nervous during the conference call, and then start sweating and trembling?*

GOOD: *What if I get really nervous during the conference call, start sweating and trembling, pee in my pants, and people avoid me the rest of my life?*

Step Two. Write the numbers one to twenty-five on a slip of paper.

Step Three. Sit, or stand, in front of a mirror so you can see yourself.

Say the worry sentence out loud, slowly, twenty-five times. After each repetition, cross the next number off your slip of paper so you can keep count.

Don't keep track of the number of repetitions in your head, because that takes too much concentration. Instead, concentrate on the actual repetitions of the worrisome thought. Go ahead and try it. Pick a time and place that allows you privacy, so you can focus your attention on what you're saying without a lot of concern for being overheard. You may feel foolish anyway, but please do give it a fair try. Don't skip past this!

All done? How did the emotional impact of the last repetition compare to the emotional impact of the first repetition? Which one bothered you more?

This exercise may not be a pleasant experience, but it will be worth the temporary pain. Experiments like this one will be very helpful in developing a better understanding of how your worry works and in cultivating a different way of responding to it.

21

REPLACE WORRY WITH PLANNING

What to Know

Worry may be one of the most tempting cognitive processes there is. For people who tend to worry, it often feels helpful to think about a problem, concern, or responsibility and invest time in anticipating potential difficulties. But if constantly focusing on your concerns tends to be self-perpetuating and activates your fight, flight, or freeze response when there isn't any real danger, is it really helping?

As we have been discussing, it can be easy to get stuck in worry, imagining one negative event after another and considering endless possible responses. You may worry about events long before it's even necessary to prepare for them and waste time deciding how to respond to imagined events that may never occur.

What to Do

Instead of getting stuck in worrying or ruminating, plan! If you anticipate that a situation you worry about will actually arise:

1. Write down any possible iterations of the situation.
2. Come up with possible solutions before moving on to other thoughts.
3. If the situation actually arises, you can put your plan in place. In the meantime, you don't need to keep thinking about it.

Here's an example: Anne's son Joey had a birthday coming up, and Anne heard that her aunt Janice would be attending his birthday party, which they'd be holding over video conference. Anne recalled a recent argument with Janice and began to worry that another argument would occur. She then got stuck in thoughts about potential conflicts with her aunt, imagining various criticisms Janice could raise and considering how she might respond. She worried about what Janice might say about her to others before she logged onto the call and started thinking of ways to respond to other people who could become involved.

Luckily, Anne had been down this route before and realized that her worries were actually producing more anxiety. She recognized that her tendency to worry was making her anticipate a big scene that might not even happen. She told herself *Stop!* and said to herself, *My plan is to get ready for the call. I'll deal with Janice later—if I need to.* When the day of the birthday party video call came, Anne's aunt seemed primarily focused on little Joey, and her conversations with Anne related to events going on in her own children's lives. In the end, Anne's recognition of her tendency to worry and her decision to interrupt it and make a plan saved her a great deal of unnecessary anxiety.

PART III

ADVANCED RELAXATION SKILLS

22

THE MINDFULNESS POWER UP

What to Know

Anxiety has the ability to hijack your mind, dominate your conscious awareness, and take over your life. But what if you could find a way to use your brain to look at your anxiety, seeing it from a distance rather than living in it and being trapped by its influence? What if you could use your brain to get outside the anxiety so it's just an experience you're having? Mindfulness is a brain-based technique that does exactly that.

Mindfulness is an age-old approach that's been practiced in various traditions for thousands of years, and something you actually practiced in the sitting meditation earlier in this book. In essence, mindfulness means understanding that all you ever really have is the present moment, and practicing a new way to inhabit and observe that moment: with a focus on allowing, accepting, and being fully aware of whatever you're experiencing. This may sound simple, but it takes practice. However, this practice can be woven into your life. You can transform your typical daily experiences into opportunities to practice mindfulness as you eat breakfast, listen to the sounds in your yard, focus on walking, or concentrate on a deep breathing practice.

After you learn to focus on mindfully observing fairly neutral everyday experiences, you can turn your awareness to your anxiety. Through practice, you relax your body and train your brain to take on a non-judging attitude, an openness to what's happening that puts you in the role of peaceful, detached observer, rather than someone who's struggling with anxiety and its physical symptoms.

What to Do

The next time you feel anxiety, seek a quiet place to practice mindfulness. Let your focus be on your bodily experience, and allow your awareness of anything else to fade. If your attention wanders, simply bring it back to the experience of anxiety in your body. For example, if you feel a rush of adrenaline, consider the experience and simply allow yourself to feel it. How intense is it? What parts of your body are affected? What sensations do you have? How do the sensations change over time?

Look at your body to see if you notice signs of anxiety. Are you trembling? Are your legs trying to move? Also notice the impulses you have, perhaps to say something or to leave. Be aware of these impulses without acting on them, and observe what happens to them as you observe. Likewise, notice the thoughts that are coming into your mind. You don't have to analyze them; just let them be there. Don't judge yourself as you make these observations; simply observe. Accept your anxiety as a normal process. Let yourself experience it as it moves through you, changing over time, without fighting it or encouraging it. Simply observe.

A lot like a savings account, mindfulness works best if you commit. Try to practice mindfulness in response to anxiety for about a month, making small deposits whenever you can take even a few minutes to attend to your anxiety. You can further develop your ability to use mindfulness with anxiety by focusing on different components of your anxiety response. For example, one time you might choose to focus on how your breathing is affected, another time on your heart, another on your thoughts, and so on. Notice how your sense of your anxiety changes when you take this approach.

23

THE PENDULUM DROP

What to Know

Hypnosis is a term derived from the Greek word for sleep. In some ways, hypnosis is similar to sleep: there is a narrowing of consciousness accompanied by inertia and passivity. Hypnosis is very relaxing. But unlike sleep, you never completely lose awareness during hypnosis. While hypnotized, you are able to respond to things going on around you. Although hypnosis is usually done with eyes closed to facilitate concentration and imagination, it also can be done with the eyes open.

Hypnosis allows you to experience your thoughts and mental images as real. While you are hypnotized, you willingly suspend disbelief for the moment, just as you do when you become absorbed in a compelling fantasy or play. For instance, when you watch a violent chase scene in a movie, your mind and body respond in many ways as though you were actually participating in the chase: your muscles tense, your stomach churns, your heart rate increases, and you feel excited or scared. The brainwave patterns traced on an electroencephalogram (EEG) during hypnosis resemble the patterns that typically occur during the actual activities that the hypnotized person is imagining (participating in a chase, relaxing at the beach, playing a musical instrument, and so on).

You may think that you have never been hypnotized but, in fact, you are no stranger to hypnosis. Often, when you concentrate on something of great interest to you, you enter hypnosis without any formal induction. Daydreaming, for example, is a hypnotic state. Long-distance driving is highly conducive to hypnosis (and commonly results in amnesia for various parts of the trip). Hypnosis is actually an easy way to achieve relaxation and relief from your anxious and racing mind.

What to Do

1. To make a pendulum, tie an object like a paper clip, pen, or ring to the end of a heavy thread that's about ten inches long.
2. If possible, sit in a reclining chair or comfortable high-backed chair with support for your arms, hands, neck, and head. Choose a comfortable position with your feet flat on the floor and your legs and arms uncrossed. Loosen your clothing. You may prefer to remove contact lenses or glasses.
3. Set aside at least thirty minutes to do this exercise without being interrupted.
4. Choose something that is the opposite of your problem and hence the essence of the goal for which you are using hypnosis. For instance, if your problem is anxiety about you job status, your goal and key phrase might be "It will turn out okay" or "Relax now." You can repeat this statement slowly as your eyes close, so that the key word

becomes associated with deep relaxation.

5. Hold the thread in your dominant hand in front of you and let the pendulum dangle above the floor.

6. Ask your subconscious for permission to go into hypnosis for two minutes. If the answer is yes, your eyes will want to close.

7. As your eyes close, picture a candle flame. Take several deep breaths and allow yourself to slip into a deeper and deeper relaxation. Breathe deeply all the way down into your abdomen and feel the spreading sense of relaxation as you exhale.

8. Tell yourself that when you have entered hypnosis, your hand will relax and drop the pendulum. Count down slowly from ten to zero.

9. When you feel ready, open your eyes. Go about your day, and try to notice if you feel more relaxed than you did before.

24

FIVE-FINGER EXERCISE

What to Know

Like the previous exercise, this is a self-hypnosis practice. Self-hypnosis has been clinically effective with symptoms of insomnia, minor chronic pain, headache, nervous tics and tremors, chronic muscular tension, and minor anxiety; it is also a well-established treatment for chronic fatigue. In this book, we are using it to help you enter a state of relaxation. Research has shown significant relaxation effects can be achieved within two days. To become proficient in the skill of self-hypnosis, practice the next exercise once a day for a week.

What to Do

Memorize the following steps or record them on your smartphone to listen to later. After you have gone through them, you can use the feeling of calmness that follows to enter hypnosis.

1.   If possible, sit in a reclining chair or a comfortable high-backed chair with support for your arms, hands, neck, and head. Choose a comfortable position with your feet flat on the floor and your legs and arms uncrossed. Loosen your clothing. You may prefer to remove contact lenses or glasses.

2.   Set aside at least thirty minutes to do this exercise without being interrupted.

3.   Choose something that is the opposite of your problem and hence the essence of the goal for which you are using hypnosis. For instance, if your problem is anxiety about you job status, your goal and key phrase might be "It will turn out okay" or "Relax now." You can repeat this statement slowly at the moment your eyes close, so that the key word becomes associated with deep relaxation.

4. Take several deep breaths and allow yourself to slip into a deeper and deeper relaxation. Breathe deeply all the way down into your abdomen and feel the spreading sense of relaxation as you exhale.

5. Touch your thumb to your index finger. As you do that, go back to a time when your body felt healthy fatigue, such as just after swimming, playing tennis, jogging, or some other exhilarating physical activity.

6. Touch your thumb to your middle finger. As you do that, go back to a time when you had a loving experience. You may choose to remember a moment of sexual fulfillment, a warm embrace, or an intimate conversation.

7. Touch your thumb to your ring finger. As you do that, recall the nicest compliment you have ever received. Try to really accept it now. By accepting it, you are showing your high regard for the person who said it. You are really paying that person a compliment in return.

8.   Touch your thumb to your little finger. As you do that, go back to the most beautiful place you have ever been. Dwell there for a while.

25

AUTOGENICS

What to Know

Autogenic training has its origins in research on hypnosis conducted in the nineteenth century. Its goal is to help people put themselves into a trance that had the effect of reducing their fatigue, tension, and painful symptoms like headaches. It also helps you deal more effectively with your everyday life. People usually report that when their fatigue and tension lifted, they felt warm and heavy. So the goal of autogenic practices is to feel warm and heavy.

Essentially, all you have to do is relax, be undisturbed, sit in a comfortable position, and concentrate passively on verbal suggestions about warmth and heaviness in your limbs.

What to Do

1. Choose a quiet room where you won't be disturbed.
2. Keep the room temperature at a moderately warm, comfortable level.
3. Keep external stimuli to a minimum.
4. Turn the lights down low.
5. Wear loose clothing.
6. Sit in an armchair in which your head, back, and extremities are supported and you are as comfortable as possible. Or sit on a stool, slightly stooped over, with your arms resting on your thighs, your neck relaxed, and your hands draped between your knees. Or lie down on your back with your head supported and your legs about eight inches apart, your toes pointed slightly outward, and your arms resting comfortably at your sides but not touching your body.
7. Take a second to notice how you're feeling in your body, beginning at the top of your head

and slowly moving down to your toes, to be sure that the position you chose is tension-free. In particular, look for overextension of your limbs such as unsupported arms, head, or legs, tightening of the limbs at the joints, or a crooked spine. If any of these overextensions exist, continue moving and supporting your body until you are well supported and comfortable, with no overextensions.

8. Close your eyes or pick a point in front of you to softly focus on.

9. Take a few slow, deep, and relaxing breaths before you begin to repeat the following statements.

Say to yourself, *My right arm is heavy ... My right arm is heavy ... My right arm is heavy ... My right arm is heavy. This should take you about half a minute. Then you would say to yourself, My left arm is heavy ... My left arm is heavy ... My left arm is heavy ... My left arm is heavy ... Then, Both of my arms are heavy ... Both of my arms are heavy ... Both of my arms are heavy ... Both of my arms are heavy* ... The entire set should take you less than four minutes. If you are recording this, be sure to leave about half a minute between each part for silent repetition.

As you silently repeat each line, passively concentrate on the part of the body it refers to. When you're finished with these lines, move to another part of your body and continue the repetition: "My [body part] is/are heavy." In other words, just notice what happens without harboring any expectations or judgments. Passive concentration does not mean spacing out or going to sleep.

Below is the full sequence of statements for this autogenic practice.

Part 1:

> *My right arm is heavy.*
> *My left arm is heavy.*
> *Both of my arms are heavy.*
> *My right leg is heavy.*
> *My left leg is heavy.*
> *Both of my legs are heavy.*
> *My arms and legs are heavy.*

Part 2:

My right arm is warm.
My left arm is warm.
Both of my arms are warm.
My right leg is warm.
Both of my legs are warm.
My arms and legs are warm.

Part 3

My right arm is heavy and warm.
Both of my arms are heavy and
warm.
Both of my legs are heavy and
warm.
My arms and legs are heavy and
warm.
It breathes me.
My heartbeat is calm and regular.

Part 4

My right arm is heavy and warm.
My arms and legs are heavy and
warm.
It breathes me.
My heartbeat is calm and regular.

My solar plexus is warm.

Part 5

My right arm is heavy and warm.
My arms and legs are heavy and warm.
It breathes me.
My heartbeat is calm and regular.
My solar plexus is warm.
My arms and legs are warm.
My forehead is cool.

At first, you will not be able to maintain perfect passive concentration. Your mind will wander. That's natural. When you find this happening, just return to script as soon as possible. When you are ready to stop the practice, say to yourself, *When I open my eyes, I will feel refreshed and alert.* Then open your eyes and breathe a few deep breaths as you stretch and flex your arms.

26

ANTI-STRESS COMBOS

What to Know

In this book, you have learned many techniques to find calm in this very moment despite the swirls of chaos around you. The best part about many of these relaxation techniques is that they can actually be combined together. Breathing and visualization are each examples. Any of the relaxation techniques from earlier in this book can be combined as you see fit, and they can also be used in conjunction with any of the anxiety and worry techniques, especially if you try to relax before doing the anxiety exercise. Here are a few exercises that combine what you have already tried and can help promote deeper relaxation.

What to Do

This first exercise combines the relaxing benefits of diaphragmatic breathing with the curative value of positive hypnotic suggestion.

1. Lie down on the floor on a rug or blanket.

2. Place your hands gently on your solar plexus (the point where your ribs start to separate above your abdomen) and practice deep, diaphragmatic breathing for a few minutes.

3. Imagine energy is rushing into your lungs with each incoming breath of air and being immediately stored in your solar plexus. Imagine that this energy is flowing out to all parts of your body with each exhalation. Form a mental picture of this energizing process.

4. Continue doing this exercise on a daily basis for at least five to ten minutes a day.

Here is another combination technique that pulls together natural deep breathing and positive visualization.

1. Begin by taking slow, deep abdominal breaths. Become aware of your growing feeling of relaxation as each deep breath expands your diaphragm.

2. Visualize a beach. See the waves rolling up the sand, the seagulls wheeling overhead, a few puffs of fleecy clouds. Hear the roar of waves and then the quiet. Hear the alternating roar, quiet, roar, quiet. Over the ocean sound you can hear the seagulls calling. Now feel the warm sand. Imagine it covering your body, warm and heavy. Really feel the weight of the sand on your arms and legs. Feel surrounded by warmth and comfort.

3. While visualizing the sand, continue to breathe as deeply as feels comfortable. Notice the rhythm of your breath. As you breathe in, say the word "warm" to yourself. Try to feel the warmth of the sand around your body. As you breathe out, say the word

"heavy." Experience the weight of the sand on your limbs. Continue your deep breathing, thinking *warm* as you inhale and *heavy* as you exhale. Continue for at least five minutes. (Note: If after a time you feel more comfortable shifting to shallower breathing, allow yourself to do so.)

27

TAKE IN THE GOOD

What to Know

Scientists believe that your brain has a built-in negativity bias. This is because, as our ancestors dodged sticks and chased carrots over millions of years of evolution, the sticks had the greater urgency and impact on survival. This negativity bias shows up in lots of ways. For example, studies have found that:

- The brain generally reacts more to a negative stimulus than to an equally intense positive one.
- Animals—including us—typically learn faster from pain than from pleasure; once burned, twice shy.
- Painful experiences are usually more memorable than pleasurable ones.
- Most people will work harder to avoid losing something they have than they'll work to gain the same thing.

- Lasting, good relationships typically need at least a 5:1 ratio of positive to negative interactions.

In your own mind, what do you usually think about at the end of the day? The fifty things that went right, or the one that went wrong? Such as the driver who cut you off in traffic, or the one thing on your To Do list that didn't get done...

In effect, the brain is like Velcro for negative experiences, but Teflon for positive ones. That shades *implicit memory*—your underlying feelings, expectations, beliefs, inclinations, and mood—in an increasingly negative direction. This is not fair, because most of the facts in your life are probably positive or at least neutral. Besides the injustice of it, the growing pile of negative experiences in implicit memory naturally makes a person more anxious, irritable, and blue—plus it gets harder to be patient and giving toward others.

But you don't have to accept this bias! By tilting *toward* the good—toward that which brings more happiness and benefit to oneself and others—you merely level the playing field. Then, instead of positive experiences washing through you like water through a sieve, they'll collect in implicit memory deep down in your brain.

You'll still see the tough parts of life. In fact, you'll become more able to change them or bear them if you take in the good, because doing so will you help put challenges in perspective, lift your energy and spirits, highlight useful resources, and fill up your own cup so you have more to offer to others. In addition to being good for adults, taking in the good is great for children, too. It helps them to become more resilient, confident, and happy, so feel free to share this practice with your whole family!

What to Do

Look for good facts, and turn them into good experiences. Good facts include positive events—like finishing a batch of e-mails or getting a compliment—and positive aspects of the world and yourself. Most good facts are ordinary and relatively minor, but they are still real. You are not looking at the world through rose-colored glasses, but simply recognizing something that is actual and true.

Then, when you're aware of a good fact—either something that currently exists or has happened in the past—let yourself *feel* good about it. So often in life a good thing happens—flowers are blooming, someone is nice, a goal's been attained—and you know it, but you don't feel it. This time, let the good fact affect you.

Be aware of any reluctance toward having positive experiences, such as thinking that you don't deserve it; that it's selfish, vain, or shameful to feel pleasure; or that if you feel good, you will lower your guard and let bad things happen. Then turn your attention back to the good facts. Keep opening up to them, breathing and relaxing, letting them move your needle. It's like sitting down to a meal: don't just look at it—taste it!

Really enjoy the experience. Most of the time, a good experience is pretty mild, and that's fine. Simply stay with it for ten, twenty, even thirty seconds in a row—instead of getting distracted by something else. Soften and open around the experience; let it fill your mind; give over to it in your body. The longer that something is held in awareness and the more emotionally stimulating it is—the more neurons that fire and thus wire together—the stronger the trace in your implicit memory.

In this practice, you are not clinging to positive experiences, because that would lead to tension and disappointment. Actually, you are doing the opposite: by taking them in, you will feel better fed inside. Your happiness will become more unconditional, increasingly based on an inner fullness rather than on external conditions.

Intend and sense that the good experience is sinking in to you. People do this in different ways. Some feel the good in the body as a warm glow spreading through the chest like the warmth of a cup of hot cocoa on a cold wintry day. Others visualize things like a golden syrup sinking down inside; a child might imagine a jewel going into a treasure chest in his or her heart. And some might simply know that, while this good experience is held in awareness, its related neural networks are busily firing and wiring together.

Any single time of taking in the good will usually make just a little difference. But over time those little differences will add up, gradually weaving positive experiences into the fabric of your brain and your whole being. In particular, as you do the practices in this book—or engage any process of psychological healing and growth, or spiritual development—really take in the fruits of your efforts. Help them stick to your mental/neural ribs!

PART IV

SUPER EFFECTIVE STRATEGIES THAT TAKE A LITTLE MORE TIME

28

SEE THE GOOD IN YOURSELF

What to Know

There is good in every person, but it's often easier to see it in others than in yourself. For example, think about a friend: What do you like about them? Include qualities such as sense of humor, fairness, honesty, intelligence, patience, passion, helpfulness, curiosity, determination, talent, spunk, or a good heart. Recognizing these positive characteristics in your friend feels reassuring, comfortable, and hopeful. It's good to recognize what's good in someone. Including you!

Each of us is like a mosaic with lots of lovely tiles. Some that are basically neutral, and a few could use a little—ah—work. It's important to see the whole mosaic. But because of the brain's bias toward negative thoughts, we tend to fixate on what's wrong with ourselves instead of what's right. If you do twenty things in a day and nineteen go fine, what's the one you think about? Probably the one that didn't go so well.

Your brain builds new structures primarily based on what you pay attention to; remember, neurons that fire together, wire together. Focusing on the "bad" tiles in the mosaic you are reinforces an underlying sense of being mediocre, flawed, or less than others. And it blocks the development of the confidence and self-worth that come from recognizing the good tiles. These results of the negativity bias are not fair. But they're sure powerful, and a big reason most of us have feelings of inadequacy or self-doubt.

Knowing your own strengths and virtues is just a matter of seeing yourself accurately. Once you see yourself accurately, you can recognize the good in yourself. This will help you feel better inside, reach out to others with less fear of rejection, and pursue your dreams with more confidence that you'll have success.

What to Do

Pick one good thing about yourself. Maybe you are particularly friendly, open, conscientious, imaginative, warm, perceptive, or steadfast. Be aware of the experience of that positive characteristic. Explore its body sensations, its emotional tones, and any attitudes or viewpoints that go with it.

Take a little time to register that you do indeed have this good quality. Let yourself become convinced of it. Look for signs of this quality for a day or a week—and feel it when you find it.

Notice any difficulty in accepting that you have this good quality, such as thoughts like *But I'm not that way all the time.* Or *But I have bad parts, too.* Try to get on your own side here and see yourself realistically, including your good qualities. It's okay that you don't live from those qualities every minute of every day. That's what it means to be a mosaic; that's what it means to be human. Repeat this process for other strengths or virtues that you have.

Now, open to the good things that others recognize in you. Start with a friend and look at yourself through their eyes. What does that person like about you? What do they appreciate, enjoy, respect, or admire? If your friend were telling someone else about your good qualities, what might they say? Do this again with several other people from different parts—and perhaps times—of your life, such as other friends or a family member, partner, teacher, coach, or coworker. Then allow other people's knowing of your good characteristics to become your own. Soften your face and body and mind to take in this knowing of the truth, the whole truth, of your personal mosaic.

Whether it starts with your own recognition of yourself or it comes from other people, let the knowing of good things about you become feelings of worth, confidence, happiness, and peace. Sense a quiet voice inside you, coming from your own core, firmly and honestly listing some of your good qualities. Listen to it. Let what it's saying sink in. If you like, write down the list and go over it from time to time; you don't have to show it to anyone.

As you go through life, look for examples of your decency, endurance, caring, and other good qualities. When you see these facts, open to feeling good about yourself. Let these times of feeling good about yourself gradually fill your heart and your days.

29

THINK THE THOUGHT—WITH A TWIST

What to Know

Start by calling to mind the absolute worst thought you can stand. Because this thought will certainly frighten or disgust you, try inviting the thought to enter your awareness in a slightly altered way. Stay connected to the thought while accepting and allowing the feeling to remain.

What to Do

Here are some ways that you can practice having your most uncomfortable thoughts with a bit of change. And remember, humor is your best ally during practice.

- Sing the thought to the tune of "Happy Birthday" or "Twinkle, Twinkle, Little Star."
- Write the thought over and over.
- Make a poem of the thought.
- Draw or paint the thought.
- Record the thought and play it back.
- Elaborate the thought into a full script with a terrible ending. (*Read it over and over.*)
- Write the thought on sticky notes and paste them all over the house (the mirror, the fridge, your purse).
- Translate the thought to another language.
- Say the words backward.
- Carry the written thought around in your pocket or tucked inside your clothing.
- Stand in front of a mirror and speak the thought out loud, over and over.
- Try to make the thought even worse—to the point of absurdity.
- Add the phrase *I am having the thought that ...* to the thought, or *I am seeing the image of ...* to the image, and repeat it on each step

as you go up and down the stairs in your home or any time you encounter stairs.

30

GET EXCITED

What to Know

Excitement is energy plus positive emotion, and it is part of joy, passion, and having fun. Some forms of excitement may be mild but still move your needle. For example, perhaps, on your personal 0-10 "thrillometer," seeing the stars on a clear night is about a 2 while the San Francisco Giants winning the World Series is a 10. Both are still exciting, just in different ways and to different degrees.

When you consider excitement in this expanded way, what moves your own needle, even a little bit? How about the sound of bagpipes, a child's first steps, traveling someplace new, finishing a project that's gone well, dancing, laughing, finding something you've wanted on super-sale, or hearing a neat idea? Of course it's hard, if not impossible, to feel excitement if you are ill or psychologically burdened. The inability to get excited is a sign that something's not right.

Under normal conditions, without excitement about *something,* life can feel flat, bland, and inert. Passion helps ignite and sustain creativity, entrepreneurship, political action, and committed relationships. Getting excited about something together is *bonding;* shared enthusiasm makes a movie, concert, political rally, conversation, or lovemaking a lot more rewarding.

As you grew up, your natural liveliness may have been criticized, dampened, or squelched. In particular, passion is woven into both strong emotions and sex; if either of these has been shamed or numbed, so has excitement. Did any of this happen to you? If it did, then gradually making more room for passion in your life—more room for delight, eagerness, and energy—is a joyful way to express yourself more fully.

What to Do

Find something that excites you, even just a bit. Feel the enjoyment in it. See if you can intensify the experience through a quick inhalation, a sense, perhaps, of energy rising in your body. Lift your chest and head, and let more aliveness come into your face. Register this feeling of excitement and make room for it in your body. Then, as you go through your day, notice what moves your own thrillometer, particularly in subtle ways. Look for things to get excited about!

Tell yourself that it's okay to get excited, thrilled, or aroused. Take a stand for a life that's got some juiciness in it. Reflect on your passions as a younger person: *What's happened to them? Should you dust one of them off and recommit to it?* Pick a part of your life that's become static, perhaps stale—such as cooking, a job, housework, repetitive parts of parenting, or even sex—and really pursue ways to pep it up. Try new dishes, turn up the music, get goofy, dance with the baby, vary your routines, and so on.

Be aware of ways you might be putting a damper on excitement, such as tightening your body, deadening your feelings, or murmuring thoughts like,

Don't stand out ... Don't be "too much" for people ... Don't be uncool. As you become more mindful of the wet blankets in your own mind, they'll dry out.

Consider some of the practices for raising energy from yoga, martial arts, or other forms of physical training. These include taking multiple deep breaths (not to the point of lightheadedness), sensing energy in the core of your body a few inches below the navel, jumping up and down a few times, making deep guttural sounds (don't try this at work!), or visualizing bright light.

Join with the excitement of others. Focus on something that lights up a friend or your partner, and look for things that could be fun, enlivening, or interesting about it to you. Don't fake anything, but nudge your own energy upwards; get more engaged with the other person's passion, which may ignite your own.

Don't rain on other people's parade—and don't let them rain on yours. Sure, if you're getting too revved up, read the social signals and either dial down your energy or take it elsewhere. But be aware that excitement makes some people uncomfortable. Sometimes, to keep their own passions bottled up, they put a lid on those of others. And honestly, that's their problem, not yours. With this sort of person, you may need to disengage, find others who share your interests, and walk to the beat of your own drummer.

Ultimately, the essence of excitement is *enthusiasm*—whose root meaning is quite profound: "moved by something extraordinary, even divine."

31

COGNITIVE DEFUSION

What to Know

Cognitive fusion means accepting that our thoughts or feelings as true even though there's no evidence, or only weak evidence, to support them, and it's very common. In American culture in particular, we generally don't question our assumptions and interpretations, but sometimes it's healthy to get outside our perspective, especially when it comes to distressing situations. Knowing that our assumptions are fallible is an important recognition, because when we're mistaken and our thoughts don't match up to reality, cognitive fusion can lead to a great deal of unnecessary anxiety.

Consider Arrianna, who had trouble contacting her boyfriend one afternoon and began to worry that something bad had happened to him. She had images of him being in the hospital and also thoughts that he was contemplating breaking up with her. As she considered these possibilities, she became very upset. Later, Arrianna found out that her boyfriend had left his phone at home and hadn't received her messages. This was a huge relief to her. What's interesting in this story is that Arrianna reacted to the thoughts she was having as if they were actual events, and those thoughts made her anxious. Do you ever catch yourself doing something similar?

When certain anxiety-igniting thoughts are combined with cognitive fusion, the risk of creating anxiety becomes greater. If you have a tendency to have pessimistic thoughts or to worry, you'll benefit from resisting cognitive fusion. For instance, if you tend to be a pessimistic thinker, it can be helpful to remind yourself that your thoughts don't determine what happens.

What to Do

A common example of cognitive fusion is believing that a situation is dangerous because it feels dangerous, even though there's no evidence of a threat. Take some time now to make a list of situations where you may be engaging in cognitive fusion. Here are some examples to get you going: *I think my neighbors criticize my lawn. Nobody at this party likes me. I absolutely cannot bear to have another panic attack.* Once you've compiled your list, review it and consider how a belief in these unfounded thoughts may be contributing to your anxiety.

Your brain is a busy, noisy place, often full of ideas and feelings. The problem isn't the ideas and feelings themselves, but a tendency to take them as absolute reality. Psychologist Steven Hayes has suggested that "it is the tendency to take these experiences literally and then to fight against them that is ... most harmful," and he offers cognitive defusion as the solution to this very common tendency. The opposite of cognitive fusion, *cognitive defusion* involves taking a different stance toward your thoughts: being aware of them without getting caught up in them.

The key to cognitive defusion is finding a way to simply recognize the different experiences you are having, as you're having them, without taking your thoughts about that situation at face value. It sounds complicated, but it's actually pretty simple. For instance, you could acknowledge a thought without buying into it by saying something like, *Hmm ... interesting. Once again I see that I'm having the thought that I'm never going to get my diploma.*

To be successful at cognitive defusion, you need to develop a sense of yourself that doesn't get lost in all the different thoughts that race through your head. The goal is to become an observer of your thoughts, not a believer in them. To help distance yourself from a thought, you could tell yourself something like, *I need to be careful of this pesky thought. I have no reason to put faith in it, and it's likely to stress me out.* Mindfulness techniques, which you practiced earlier, are also very helpful, as they help you build strength and skill in focusing your thoughts on what you choose and resisting the urge to get lost in thoughts that may or may not reflect reality.

32

BEAT EXHAUSTION AND FIND STRENGTH

What to Know

To make your way in life—to enjoy the beautiful things it offers, steer clear of hazards, and find friendship and love—you need strength. Not chest-thumping pushiness, but determination and grit. Strength comes in many forms, including endurance and restraint. For example, if you want to move a boat at the edge of a dock, don't run into it with a big smash; you'll just hurt yourself. Instead, stand on the edge of the dock, put your hand on the boat, and lean into it. *The strength is in continuing to lean.*

Inner strength, or mental strength, is not all or nothing. You can build it, just like a muscle. Mental strength draws on physical health, which is fueled by: eating protein at every meal; taking vitamin and mineral supplements daily; exercising several times a week; setting aside seven to nine hours a day for sleep; using intoxicants in moderation or not at all; and addressing and resolving chronic health problems, even seemingly mild ones. If you are not doing these, how about starting today?

What to Do

Make a list of your strengths, such as intelligence, honesty, and resilience. Be accurate—not unfairly self-critical. Recognizing your strengths will help you feel stronger. If it's appropriate, ask someone what he or she thinks some of your strengths are.

Think about some of the good things you use your strengths for, such as earning a living, raising a family, growing as a person, or making our world better. Tell yourself, *It is good for me to be strong. My strength helps good things happen. Good people want me to be strong;anyone who wants me to be weak is not on my side.* Notice any beliefs that it is bad to be strong ... and then turn your attention back to the good reasons for being strong.

To increase your sense of strength still further, recall times you felt strong. What did your body feel like then? What was your posture, point of view, or intention? Explore embodying strength right now: maybe lifting your chin, widening your stance, or breathing deeply. Take in these physical sensations and attitudes of strength so you can tap into them again.

Notice how good it feels to be strong. Feel the pleasure in your body, perhaps a quiet fierceness and resolve. Enjoy the confidence that strength brings, the sense of possibility. Appreciate how your strength empowers your caring, protectiveness, and love.

Tell yourself that you are strong. That you can endure, persist, cope, and prevail. That you are strong enough to hold your experience in awareness without being overwhelmed. That the winds of life can blow, and blow hard, but you are a deeply rooted tree, and winds just make you even stronger.

And when they are done blowing, there you still stand. Offering shade and shelter, flowers and fruit. Strong and lasting.

33

USE EXERCISE TO COPE WITH ANXIETY

What to Know

The fight, flight, or freeze response is programmed into your brain. Instead of resisting your body's preparations to fight or flee from the things that feel threatening, why not look for opportunities to work with that instinct and utilize your muscles in ways that will make you less reactive to stress, worry, and anxiety?

Brief periods of aerobic exercise can be very effective in reducing muscle tension. If you run or walk briskly when you feel anxious, you'll make use of muscles that have been prepared for action. This will lower levels of adrenaline and use up glucose released into the bloodstream by your body's stress response. And after you exercise, you'll experience substantial, long-lasting muscle relaxation.

In fact, if you anticipate that a particular event or phase of your day may amp up your anxiety, a carefully timed exercise routine may allow you to get through it with less anxiety. In other words, you may be able to achieve a tranquilizing effect without taking tranquilizers. Exercise doesn't just reduce anxiety in the moment or for a few hours afterward. Research shows that following a regular exercise program for at least ten weeks can reduce people's general level of anxiety.

The best type of exercise for you, both physically and mentally, is exercise that meets the following four criteria:

• You enjoy doing it.
• You'll keep doing it.
• It's moderately intense.
• Your doctor approves it.

This means you should choose one or two types of exercise to engage in at least three times a week for thirty minutes each time. Whatever you choose, remember that getting your heart pumping and your blood flowing has many benefits. Once you feel the improvement in your mood and reductions in your overall stress level, you should find it easier to stick with an exercise program.

What to Do

This brief exercise will help you assess your current exercise patterns and strengthen your commitment to a regular, long-term program of physical activity. Take some time to consider all of the following questions:

- *How often do you exercise each week, and how long does each period of exercise last?*
- *If you don't exercise regularly, would you consider beginning an exercise program to decrease the nervous activation that anxiety creates?*
- *Which type of exercise most appeals to you?*

After reflecting on what kind of exercise you already enjoy or might find appealing, use a day planner or reminder board to schedule out when you will exercise. If you tend to have certain days of the week that cause more stress and anxiety than others, make sure to set aside some time on those days to move your body and disperse that anxious energy.

Lastly, right before exercising, take a moment to notice your breath and feel whatever anxious thoughts are racing around in your brain. On a scale from 1 to 10, rate your levels of anxiety pre-workout. Then, when you are done exercising, take a moment again to pause and reflect on how you feel. Ask yourself, *Do I feel less anxious after exercise?* Taking stock of what regular exercise can do for your overall mood is an important tool in managing your anxiety right now. Not to mention it gives you a little extra motivation to stick to an exercise habit.

34

GET SOME SLEEP

What to Know

Most people know how much more refreshed and alert they feel when they've gotten a good night's sleep, but few truly grasp how important sleep is for the brain. People tend to see sleep as a period in which the brain shuts down, but sleep is actually a very active time for the brain. Just like your heart or immune system, your brain continues to work while you sleep. In fact, during certain periods of sleep, your brain is even more active than when you're awake. As you sleep, your brain is busy making sure that hormones are released, needed neurochemicals are produced, and memories are stored.

Many people are also unaware that sleepless nights have detrimental effects on their health, as well as their brain. Don't assume that you're getting enough sleep if you don't feel tired. When you're sleep deprived, you can still feel alert or even energetic in stimulating situations. And because anxious people are often in an alert state, they may not feel sleepy and therefore assume that they aren't sleep deprived. It may be that they are and just don't recognize it. Be aware that sleep deprivation can show up in many forms, including increased anxiety or irritability, difficulty concentrating, or lack of motivation.

What to Do

To help you determine whether you have sleep problems, read through the statements below and check any that are true for you:

- I'm often restless and find it difficult to fall asleep when I go to bed.
- I've used medications or alcohol to help me sleep.
- I need complete silence to sleep. Any noise will prevent me from relaxing.
- It often takes me more than twenty minutes to fall asleep.
- I often feel drowsy, fall asleep, or nap during the day.

- I don't go to bed or wake up at a consistent time.
- I awaken too early and can't get back to sleep.
- I don't sleep soundly. I just can't relax.
- When I get out of bed in the morning, I don't feel rested.
- I dread trying to go to sleep at night.
- I depend on caffeine to get me through the day.

The more of these statements you check, the more likely it is that you have sleep debt. *Sleep debt* occurs when people haven't been getting as much sleep as they need and the hours of missed sleep start accumulating. Most adults need between seven and nine hours of sleep per night. Each night you miss an hour or so of sleep, your debt grows. So even if you get enough sleep on a given night, you may still feel sleepy or irritable the next day as a result of an accumulated sleep debt.

As you work on getting adequate sleep, it's important to understand when REM sleep occurs. REM sleep occurs later in the sleep cycle, and phases of

REM sleep become more frequent at the end of the overall sleep period. Many people don't realize that a long period of sleep is necessary for getting into these stages of REM sleep. Therefore, four hours of sleep followed by an hour of wakefulness and then another four hours of sleep isn't equal to eight hours of sleep.

When you return to sleep after being awake for even just half an hour, the sleep cycles start over from the beginning, so it will take many more hours to get through an entire sleep period. It isn't like returning to watching a movie where you left off. It's like having to go through the whole movie again from the beginning.

More to Do

After reading this information about sleep, you may be thinking, *I want to get good sleep, but it isn't easy!* Of course, our current twenty-four-hour culture—with media, shopping, and restaurants available at all hours—can keep us from getting sufficient sleep on a regular basis. Certain stages of life also make one vulnerable to sleep deprivation, including the college years or the first months of parenthood.

To calm anxiety, you need to resist influences that interfere with sleep. However, anxiety itself often impairs people's ability to sleep, with difficulty falling asleep or early awakening both being quite common. When coping with these difficulties, it's useful to know which approaches will help and which will actually worsen the problem. The best approach to improving sleep is to take a careful look at your sleep-related routines to make sure that they're healthy.

The following sleeping practices can really assist you in achieving a good night's sleep:

- Before you go to bed, practice a routine set of relaxing rituals. Eliminate light stimulation for at least an hour before bed.
- Exercise during the day.
- Establish a consistent bedtime and waking time.
- Avoid napping.
- Near bedtime, replace activating thoughts with relaxing ones.

- If worries haunt you at bedtime, schedule a worry time during the day.
- Ensure that your sleeping environment is conducive to sleep.
- Avoid caffeine, alcohol, and spicy foods in the late afternoon and evening.
- Use relaxing breathing techniques to prepare for sleep.
- If you can't fall asleep after thirty minutes in bed, get up and do something relaxing.
- Use your bed primarily for sleep.
- Avoid using sleep aids.

35

SEND ANXIETY TO THE SPAM FOLDER

What to Know

Imagine that you are walking down the street, on your way to your car, and a complete stranger walks by you and utters a disgusting comment, and then keeps on walking. You could decide to engage him by saying something back (perhaps "How dare you!" or "That's disgusting"), but then he would have your attention. He might then say something else or even get aggressive. Most of you would agree that the best bet is to keep on walking. Don't even let him know that you heard him. Act as if you couldn't care less. Of course you know it occurred, and your feelings are also undeniable, but the best way to minimize the event is to not get involved.

Why would you act that way? *Not because you agree or think it is true.*

But because you know it reduces the likelihood the person will continue his harangue. So you may very well feel frightened or upset, but you will try to act as if you are ignoring the comment. Push back, and you are increasing the chances of another comment.

Anxiety, with its intrusive thoughts, works very much the same way. When you respond to anxious thoughts by judging them, arguing with them, or seeking reassurance to combat them, you become entangled with them. Entanglement can happen in a variety of ways, but most often answering back or arguing with an intrusion is what keeps it going. Getting involved and entangled with unwanted anxious thoughts only makes them stronger and more insistent.

What to Do

Imagine that you open the following email addressed to you:

Congratulations! This is your lucky day. Your third cousin twice removed, who was the head of the [insert foreign country] *Diamond Industry,* *has died and left $14, 000, 000, 000 to you. In order to collect this inheritance, please click on this link and provide us with your bank routing number. We will immediately transfer into your account the sum of $14, 000, 000, 000. Again, accept our sincere congratulations.*

Would you start excitedly imagining what it would be like to buy your own yacht, own your own private jet, or buy your own island? We hope not, of course, because the words in this communication are not to be believed. The content is immaterial. This is a scam, not an inheritance notice.

When you push the "send to spam" button on any number of emails just like this, you have already disentangled yourself from the *content* of the email. You have no problem buying the idea that the words should not be believed, and the email is communicating a very different message: "Send me your money, sucker!"

Remember the lesson from the very beginning of this book: *thoughts are not facts.* Thoughts are imaginations inside your mind. You could almost say that thoughts are a form of pretending, especially when those thoughts are telling you that something is dangerous when you know very well that it isn't. So, when you find yourself getting entangled with an anxious thought, do your best to come back to the realization that thoughts aren't facts, and remember that anxiety is bluffing you once again. Then send that anxious thought to the spam folder so that your mind can get back to things you actually care about.

36

COPING THOUGHTS

What to Know

Coping thoughts are thoughts or statements that are likely to have positive effects on your emotional well-being. One way of evaluating the usefulness of thoughts is to look at the effects they have on you. In this light, you can clearly see the value of coping thoughts, which are more likely to result in calm responses and an increased ability to cope with difficult situations.

What to Do

Take a look at the following chart. In the left column you will see (and maybe recognize) some of the anxious thoughts that a lot of us have. In the right column, you will see "coping thoughts" tailored for each of these anxious thoughts.

It's no use trying. Things will never go back to normal.	I'm going to try, regardless because then there's at least a chance that I can find more fulfillment in life despite the circumstances.
Something's going to go wrong. I can feel it.	I don't know what's going to happen. These kinds of feelings have been wrong before.
I need to focus on this thought, doubt, or concern to figure out the exact right way to proceed.	I've spent too much time on this and I need to move on. There won't be any exact right way to proceed, I'll just manage the best I can.
I must be competent and excel at juggling school, work, and motherhood all at the same time.	No one is perfect. I'm human and I expect I'll make mistakes at times.
Everyone should like me.	No one is liked by everyone, so I'll encounter people who don't like me.
I can't stand being stuck at home during this pandemic!	I have been through more difficult things. I'll survive.
I can't help worrying about whether I am infected or not.	Worrying won't change if I have it or not. It only upsets me.
I don't want to disappoint the people I work with.	Trying to please everyone is impossible. Especially when all of us are struggling to work from home. Let it go.

I can't handle going to a store right now.	I'm a competent person, and even though I feel a little unsafe, I can get through it.

If you saw, in the left column, an anxious thought that you have, or if one of yours comes to mind while reading the examples, take a moment to brainstorm a positive coping thought for yourself. Write your coping thought down in your phone so you can look at it next time that anxious thought creeps up on you. Of course, you'll have to be vigilant about recognizing anxious thoughts and substituting coping thoughts, but it's worth the effort. Be sure to focus on the types of thoughts that are most problematic for you. For example, if you tend toward perfectionism, it's useful to watch for "musts" and "shoulds" in your thinking.

When you tell yourself you "must" accomplish something or that something "should" happen according to a certain plan or schedule, you're setting yourself up for stress and worry. The words "must" and "should" make it seem like a rule is being violated if your performance is less than perfect or if events don't unfold as planned. If nothing else, replace "I should..." with "I'd like to..." That way, you aren't creating a rule that must be followed. Instead, you're simply expressing a goal or a desire—one that may or may not be met. It's a kinder, gentler thought.

37

BE GENEROUS

What to Know

Giving—to others, to the world, to oneself—is deep in our nature as human beings.

When our mammalian ancestors first appeared about two hundred million years ago, their capacities for bonding, emotion, and generosity were extraordinary evolutionary breakthroughs. Unlike reptiles and fish, mammals and birds care for their young, pair bond (sometimes for life), and usually form complex social groups organized around various kinds of cooperation. This takes more smarts than, say, a fish laying a swarm of eggs and swimming away—so in proportion to body weight, mammals and birds have bigger brains than reptiles and fish do.

When primates came along about 60 million years ago, there was another jump in brain size based on the "reproductive advantages" of social abilities. The primate species that are the most relational—that have the most complex communications, grooming, alpha/beta hierarchies, and so on—have the largest cortex (in proportion to weight).

Then early hominids emerged, starting to make stone tools about 2.5 million years ago. Since then, the brain has tripled in size, and much of this new cortex is devoted to interpersonal skills such as language, empathy, attachment to family and friends, romance, cooperative planning, and altruism. As the brain enlarged, a longer childhood was required to allow for its growth after birth and to make good use of its wonderful new capabilities. This necessitated more help from fathers than was necessary in the ancient past to keep children and their mothers alive during the uniquely long juvenile phase of a human life, and also more help from "the village it takes to raise a child."

The bonding and nurturing of primate mothers—in a word, their *giving*—gradually evolved into romantic love, fathers as well as mothers caring for their young, friendship, and the larger web of affiliations that join humans together. Additionally, our ancestors bred mainly within their own band. Bands that were better at the give-and-take of relationships and teamwork out-competed other bands for scarce resources—so, the genes that built more socially intelligent brains proliferated in the human genome.

In sum, giving, broadly defined, both enabled and drove the evolution of the brain over millions of years.

Consequently, we swim in a sea of generosity—of many daily acts of consideration, reciprocity, benevolence, compassion, kindness, helpfulness, warmth, appreciation, respect, patience, forbearance, and contribution—but, like those proverbial fish, we often don't realize we're wet. Because of the brain's negativity bias, moments of not-giving—one's own resentments and selfishness, and the withholding and unkindness of others—pop out like blazing headlines. Moreover, modern economies can make it seem like giving and getting is largely about making money, but that part of life is just a tiny fraction of the original and still vast "generosity economy," with its circular flows of freely given, unmonetized goods and services.

When you express your giving nature, it feels good for you, benefits others, prompts them to be good to you in turn, and adds one more lovely thread to the great tapestry of human generosity.

What to Do

Take care of yourself. Don't give in ways that harm you or others (for example, offering a blind eye to someone's alcoholism). Keep refueling yourself; it's easier to give when you feel taken care of—or at least you're not running on empty.

Prime the pump of generosity. Be aware of things you are grateful for or glad about. Bring to mind a sense of already being full, so that you'll not feel deprived or emptied out if you give a little more.

Notice that giving is natural for you. You don't need to be a saint to be a giving person. Generosity comes in many forms, including heart, time, self-control, service, food, and money. From this perspective, consider how much you already give each day. Open to feeling good about yourself as a giver.

Give your full attention. Stay present with others minute after minute, staying with their topic or agenda. You may not like what they say, but you could still offer a receptive ear. (Especially important with a child or mate.) Then, when it's your turn, the other person will likely feel better about you taking the microphone.

Offer nonreactivity. Much of the time, interactions, relationships, and life altogether would go better if we did not add our comments, advice, or emotional reactions to a situation, especially when these weren't called for. Not-doing is sometimes the best gift.

Be helpful. For example, volunteer for a food bank if you feel healthy, give money to a good cause, or increase your own housework or childcare if your partner is doing more than you.

Do your own practice. One of your best contributions to others is to raise your own level of well-being and functioning. Whatever your practice is or could grow to be, do it with a whole heart, as a daily offering to whatever you hold sacred, to your family and friends, and to the widening world.

38

LOVE

What to Know

We all want to receive love, but it doesn't always come in the form we desire. For example, perhaps someone offers romantic love but that's not what you're looking for—or maybe love doesn't come at all right now. When this happens, there is usually heartache and feelings of helplessness; human history is one long lesson that, try as we might, we can't make others love us.

This practice is about expressing love, which is distinct from receiving it. When you focus on the love you give rather than the love you get, you're working on the cause, not the effect. In other words, you're the cue ball, not the eight ball, and this sense of agency supports feelings of efficacy and self-confidence; it also boosts your mood.

Focusing on the love you give is also a form of enlightened self-interest, because the best way to get love is to give it. Even if your love isn't returned in the exact way you desire, giving love will most likely improve your relationships and calm any troubled waters in them. Sometimes people worry that being loving will make them vulnerable or drained, but you can probably see in your own experience that love itself doesn't do this. Love protects and nurtures those who give it. Ask yourself: when loving, don't you feel uplifted and stronger?

We need to give love to be healthy and whole. If you bottle up your love, you bottle up your whole being. Love is like water: it needs to flow; otherwise, it backs up on itself and gets stagnant and smelly. Look at the faces of some people who are very loving. They're beautiful, aren't they? Being loving heals old wounds inside and opens untapped reservoirs of energy and talent. It's also a profound path of awakening, playing a central role in all of the world's major religious traditions.

The world needs your love. Those you live with and work with need it. So do your family and friends, people near and far, and this whole battered planet. Never underestimate the ripples spreading out from just one loving word, thought, or deed!

What to Do

Love is as natural as breathing, yet like the breath, it can get constricted. Sometimes you may need to release it, strengthen it, and help it flow more freely with methods like these:

- Bring to mind the sense of being with people who care about you, and then open to *feeling* cared about. Let this feeling fill you, warming your heart, softening your face. Sink into this experience. It's okay if opposite thoughts arise (for example, rejection); observe them for a moment before returning to feeling cared about—which will warm up the neural circuits of being loving yourself.
- Sense into the area around your heart and think of things that evoke

heartfelt feelings such as gratitude, compassion, or kindness. To bring harmony to the tiny changes in the interval between heartbeats. Breathe such that your inhalations and exhalations are about the same length, since inhaling speeds up the heart rate and exhaling slows it down. The heart has more than a metaphorical link to love; the cardiovascular and nervous systems lace together in your body like lovers' fingers, and practices like these will nurture wholehearted well-being in you and promote greater warmth for others.

- Strengthen these loving feelings with soft thoughts toward others, such as *I wish you well. May you not be in pain. May you be at peace. May you live with ease.* If you feel upset with someone, you can include these reactions in your awareness while also extending loving thoughts like, *I'm angry with you and I won't let you hurt me again—yet I still hope you find true happiness. I wish you well.*

39

ACKNOWLEDGE AND ACCEPT

What to Know

What's to acknowledge? That you're having another worrisome thought? It might be annoying to find worry in the back of your head. You might want to refuse to acknowledge its appearance because it seems so unreasonable that, once again, this thought is occurring to you.

Maybe you've dismissed this thought many times before, yet here it is again, serving no useful purpose, bothering you like a spam email that shows up in your mailbox every hour. Or maybe, even though you've had lots of experiences with worrisome thoughts and have never been harmed by them, you still respond with fear because you wonder, *What if this time is the time something happens?* You probably wish you could be perfectly sure that the thought is false, for all time, but no one can have that degree of certainty.

What if you simply acknowledged that you're having another worrisome thought? You have a brain, so you have thoughts. Simple as that. There's no need to try to ignore the thought, to pretend it's not there. Here you are, having another one of the many, many thoughts you will have today, and this one happens to be a loser. Whom do you acknowledge this thought to? Usually just yourself, right? This acknowledgment is an internal process in which you briefly notice the presence of the worrisome thoughts, acknowledge them without resistance or suppression, and move on to the next thing.

What's to accept? The fact that you're having a thought you don't like. You may or may not agree with the content of the thought. You may find it reasonable, or you might find it repulsive. It doesn't really matter! You don't get to pick and choose which thoughts you'll have and which thoughts you won't have—nobody does! There's no need to try to contradict the thought, to disprove it, to make it go away, or to reassure yourself. There probably won't be any benefit if you do.

No one expects you to control your thoughts. You're accountable for your actions, and you'll be judged by your actions, not by your thoughts. You can have a worrisome thought, same as you can have an angry thought, a jealous thought, a sexy thought, a wacky thought, a kind thought, an unkind thought, a shameful thought, a compassionate thought, even a murderous thought, or whatever.

What to Do

This first step—acknowledge and accept—is probably the most important and powerful of the three. Here it's described as simply as possible, but that doesn't mean it's easy. Some people may be able to simply acknowledge and accept the unwanted thoughts and move on without the use of any other techniques or responses. If that works for you, great! Just move on without spending any time on this step.

Still here? Well, in order to figure out some good ways to respond to worry, it's helpful to clarify the kind of situation you're facing. You can do this by using the two-part test from earlier in this book:

1. Is there a problem that exists now in the external world around you?
2. If there is, can you do something to change it now?

If you get anything other than two yes answers, you don't have a problem in your external world that you can solve right now. Your problem is worry.

More to Do

When you find yourself facing off with worry, keep two points in mind. It might help to put these on your phone or a 3x5 card until you get in the habit of remembering.

1. What you have is the emotion of feeling nervous.
2. It's okay to feel nervous. You probably really, really dislike the emotion, but it's like the experience of sitting in an uncomfortably warm room, not like camping in the midst of a

forest fire. It's discomfort, not danger.

The problem you face is not the problem described in the catastrophe clause of your worry. Instead, it's the discomfort you experience in response to the worrisome thought, and your natural inclination to take that thought seriously. When you resist the thought with your usual selection of anti-worry responses, this is when you once again experience the difficulty of *The harder I try, the worse it gets.* However, when you acknowledge your worry and accept its inevitability, you find yourself in the opposite situation wherein *The less I try (to resist the thought), the easier it gets (to tolerate it).*

40

HAVE FAITH

What to Know

Before you close this book, we'd like you to try a little experiment. In your mind or out loud, complete this sentence a few times: "I have faith in..." Then complete another sentence a few times: "I have no faith in..." What does having faith—and having no faith—feel like?

In your experience of faith, there's probably a sense of trusting in something. This makes sense since the word "faith" comes from the Latin root "to trust." Faith comes from direct experience, reason, trusted sources, and sometimes from something that just feels deeply right and that's all you can say about it. Sometimes faith seems obvious, like expecting water to yield each time you prepare to dive in; other times, faith is more of a conscious choice—an act of faith—such as choosing to believe that your child will be all right as they leave home for college.

What do you have faith in—out there in the world or inside yourself?

Without faith out in the world and inside you, life can feel shaky and scary. Faith grounds you in what's reliable and supportive; it's the antidote to doubt and fear. It strengthens you and supports you in weathering hard times. It helps you stay on your chosen paths, with confidence that they will lead to good places. In a lovely positive cycle, faith fuels the hope and optimism that encourage the actions that lead to the results that confirm your faith in the first place. Faith lifts your eyes to the far horizons, toward what's sacred, even divine.

Sure, some skepticism is good. But going overboard with it leads to an endless loop of mistrusting the world and doubting yourself. Essentially, you need to have faith that you'll make good choices about where to have faith! This means avoiding two pitfalls:

- *Putting too much trust in the wrong places:* people who won't come through for you, a business or job that's unlikely to turn out well, dogmas and prejudices, or a habit of mind that harms you—like a guardedness with others that may have worked okay when you were young but is now like walking around in a suit of armor that's three sizes too small.

• *Putting too little trust in the right places:* the willingness of most people to hear what you really have to say, the results that will come if you keep plugging away, or the goodness inside your own heart, to name a few.

What to Do

1. Make a list of what you *do* have faith in—both in the world and in yourself. You can do this in your mind, on paper, or by talking with someone.

2. Ask yourself where your faith might be misplaced. Be sure to consider too much faith in certain aspects of your own mind, such as in beliefs that you are somehow weak or tainted, that

others don't care about you, or that somehow you're going to get different results by doing pretty much the same old things.

3. Pick one instance of misguided faith, and consciously step away from it. Reflect on how you came to develop it and what it has cost you; imagine the benefits of a life without it; and develop a different resource to replace it. Repeat these steps for other cases of misplaced faith.

4. Make another list, this one of what you *could* reasonably have faith in—in the world and in yourself. These are missed opportunities for confidence, such as in people who could be trusted more (including children), in the basic safety of most days for most people, and in your own strengths and virtues.

5. Next, pick one entry from the list above and try to have a little more faith in it. Remember the good reasons for relying upon it. Imagine how more trust in it will

help you and others. Consciously choose to believe in it.

6. Lastly, consider some of the good qualities and aspirations in your innermost heart. Give yourself over to them for a moment—or longer. What's that like?

Ultimately, try to have more faith in the best parts of yourself. They've always been faithful to you.

SUGGESTED READING

Buddha's Brain: The Practical Neuroscience of Happiness, Love & Wisdom by Rick Hanson, PhD

Just One Thing: Developing a Buddha Brain One Simple Practice at a Time by Rick Hanson, PhD

Needing to Know for Sure: A CBT-based Guide to Overcoming Compulsive Checking and Resassurance Seeking by Martin N. Seif, PhD, and Sally M. Winston, PsyD

Overcoming Unwanted Intrusive Thoughts: A CBT-based Guide to Getting Over Frightening, Obsessive, or Disturbing Thoughts by Martin N. Seif, PhD, and Sally M. Winston, PsyD

The Relaxation and Stress Reduction Workbook, 7th Edition by Martha Davis, PhD, Elizabeth Robbins Eshelman, MSW, and Matthew McKay, PhD

Rewire Your Anxious Brain: How to Use Neuroscience of Fear to End Anxiety, Panic & Worry by Catherine M. Pittman, PhD, and Elizabeth M. Karle, MLIS

Thoughts & Feelings:Taking Control of Your Moods and Your Life by Martha Davis, PhD, Matthew McKay, PhD, and Patrick Fanning

The Worry Trick: How Your Brain Tricks You Into Expecting the Worst and What You Can Do About It by David A. Carbonell, PhD

Rick Hanson, PhD, is a psychologist, senior fellow of UC Berkeley's Greater Good Science Center, and New York Times bestselling author. His books have been published in twenty-nine languages, and include *Neurodharma, Resilient, Hardwiring Happiness, Buddha's Brain, Just One Thing,* and *Mother Nurture*—with 900,000 copies printed in English alone. His free weekly newsletter has 200,000 subscribers, and his online programs have scholarships available for those with financial need. He's lectured at NASA, Google, Oxford, and Harvard, and taught in meditation centers worldwide. An expert on positive neuroplasticity, his work has been featured on BBC, CBS, NPR, and other major media. He began meditating in 1974, and is founder of the Wellspring Institute for Neuroscience and Contemplative Wisdom. He and his wife live in northern California and have two adult children. He loves wilderness and taking a break from emails.

Matthew McKay, PhD, is a professor at the Wright Institute in Berkeley, CA. He has authored and coauthored numerous books, including *Self-Esteem, The Relaxation and Stress Reduction Workbook, Thoughts and Feelings,* and *ACT on Life Not on Anger.* His books combined have sold more than four million copies. He received his PhD in clinical psychology from the California School of Professional Psychology, and specializes in the cognitive behavioral treatment of anxiety and depression.

Martha Davis, PhD, was a psychologist in the department of psychiatry at Kaiser Permanente Medical Center in Santa Clara, CA, where she practiced individual, couples, and group psychotherapy for more than thirty years prior to her retirement. She is coauthor of *Thoughts and Feelings.*

Elizabeth Robbins Eshelman, MSW, worked for the Kaiser Permanente Health Care Program for thirty-seven years. During her tenure, she was a clinical social worker, hospice director, researcher, health educator, and management development instructor and coach. She is retired and lives in Northern California.

Martin N. Seif, PhD, is cofounder of the Anxiety and Depression Association of America (ADAA), and was a member of its board of directors from 1977 through 1991. Seif is former associate director of the Anxiety and Phobia Treatment Center at White Plains Hospital, a faculty member of New York-Presbyterian Hospital, and is board certified in cognitive behavioral psychology from the American Board of Professional Psychology. He maintains a private practice in New York, NY; and Greenwich, CT; and is coauthor of *What Every Therapist Needs to Know About Anxiety Disorders* and *Overcoming Unwanted Intrusive Thoughts.*

Sally M. Winston, PsyD, is founder and codirector of the Anxiety and Stress Disorders Institute of Maryland in Towson, MD. She served as the first chair of the ADAA's Clinical Advisory Board, and received their prestigious Jerilyn Ross Clinician Advocate Award. She is a master clinician who has given sought-after workshops for therapists for decades. She is coauthor of *What Every Therapist Needs to Know About*

Anxiety Disorders and *Overcoming Unwanted Intrusive Thoughts.*

David A. Carbonell, PhD, is a clinical psychologist who specializes in treating anxiety in all its forms. He is author of *Panic Attacks Workbook, The Worry Trick,* and *Fear of Flying Workbook.* He is "coach" of the popular self-help site www.anxietycoach.com, and has taught workshops on the treatment of anxiety disorders to more than 9,000 professional psychotherapists in the U.S. and abroad. He is a long-standing member of the Anxiety and Depression Association of America, and a frequent presenter at their annual conferences. He received his doctorate in clinical psychology from DePaul University in 1985, and has maintained a practice devoted to the treatment of anxiety disorders since 1990. He lives in Chicago, IL, with his wife and a pair of rescue dogs. In his spare time, he is founding member of The Therapy Players, an improvisational comedy troupe of professional psychotherapists which performs at clubs, theaters, and mental health conferences throughout the Chicago area.

Elizabeth M. Karle, MLIS, is collection management supervisor at the Cushwa-Leighton Library at Saint Mary's College in Notre Dame, IN. In addition to supplying research for this book, she has personal experience with anxiety disorders—providing a first-hand perspective that focuses the book on what is most useful for the anxiety sufferer. Originally from Illinois, she currently resides in South Bend, IN, and holds degrees or certificates from the University of Notre Dame, Roosevelt University, and Dominican University. She is author of *Hosting a Library Mystery*.

Catherine M. Pittman, PhD, is associate professor at Saint Mary's College in Notre Dame, IN. As a licensed clinical psychologist in private practice in South Bend, IN, she specializes in the treatment of brain injuries and anxiety disorders. She is a member of the Anxiety and Depression Association of America (ADAA), and provides workshops and seminars on the topics of anxiety and stress.

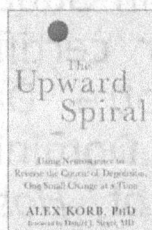

Real change is possible

For more than forty-five years, New Harbinger has published proven-effective self-help books and pioneering workbooks to help readers of all ages and backgrounds improve mental health and well-being, and achieve lasting personal growth. In addition, our spirituality books offer profound guidance for deepening awareness and cultivating healing, self-discovery, and fulfillment.

Founded by psychologist Matthew McKay and Patrick Fanning, New Harbinger is proud to be an independent, employee-owned company. Our books reflect our core values of integrity, innovation, commitment, sustainability, compassion, and trust. Written by leaders in the field and recommended by therapists worldwide, New Harbinger books are practical, accessible, and provide real tools for real change.

BACK COVER MATERIAL

YOUR EMERGENCY ANXIETY TOOL KIT

When you're experiencing high levels of stress and anxiety, you need *quick, in-the-moment* relief. Whether you're dealing with financial strains, relationship struggles, or are just feeling the weight of the world in uncertain times, it's easy to become trapped in a constant state of mental and physical exhaustion. This emergency kit has you covered.

The Anxiety First Aid Kit offers powerful tools for triaging stress and anxiety in those moments when you need it most. You'll find easy and doable ways to help you press pause on panic, and find your calm spot right away. You'll discover immediate interventions to help you relax *before* your anxiety and stress go into overdrive. And finally, you'll learn how to make healthy and workable lifestyle changes to improve your mental health and increase resilience, so you can effectively manage stressful situations in the future—no matter what life throws at you.

THIS EMERGENCY TOOL KIT INCLUDES:
- **Mindful breathing exercises**
- **Body scan meditations**
- **Relaxation techniques**
- **And much more!**

9 780369 373281